D0842676

OUR LIVING WORLD

Microorganisms:
The Unseen World

By

Edward R. Ricciuti

Series Editor: Vincent Marteka
Introduction by John Behler, *New York Zoological Society*

A B L A C K B I R C H   P R E S S   B O O K
WOODBRIDGE, CONNECTICUT

Published by Blackbirch Press, Inc.
260 Amity Road
Woodbridge, CT 06525

Printed in Canada

10 9 8 7 6 5 4

Editorial Director: Bruce Glassman
Editor: Tanya Lee Stone
Assistant Editor: Elizabeth M. Taylor
Design Director: Sonja Kalter
Production: Sandra Burr, Rudy Raccio, Madeline Parker

Library of Congress Cataloging-in-Publication Data

Ricciuti, Edward R.
    Microorganisms / by Edward R. Ricciuti; introduction by John Behler.
—1st ed.
        p.   cm. — (Our living world)
    Includes bibliographical references and index.
    ISBN 1-56711-040-1
    1. Microbiology—Juvenile literature. [1. Microorganisms.] I. Title.
II. Series.
QR57.R53   1994
576—dc20   93-44544
                                                                    CIP
                                                                    AC

Contents

What Does It Mean to Be "Alive"?

Introduction by John Behler,
New York Zoological Society

One summer morning, as I was walking through a beautiful field, I was inspired to think about what it really means to be "alive." Part of the answer, I came to realize, was right in front of my eyes.

The meadow was ablaze with color, packed with wildflowers at the height of their blooming season. A multitude of insects, warmed by the sun's early-morning rays, began to stir. Painted turtles sunned themselves on an old mossy log in a nearby pond. A pair of wood ducks whistled a call as they flew overhead, resting near a shagbark hickory on the other side of the pond.

As I wandered through this unspoiled habitat, I paused at a patch of milkweed to look for monarch-butterfly caterpillars, which depend on the milkweed's leaves for food. Indeed, the caterpillars were there, munching away. Soon these larvae would spin their cocoons, emerge as beautiful orange-and-black butterflies, and begin a fantastic 1,500-mile (2,400-kilometer) migration to wintering grounds in Mexico. It took biologists nearly one hundred years to unravel the life history of these butterflies. Watching them in the milkweed patch made me wonder how much more there is to know about these insects and all the other living organisms in just that one meadow.

The patterns of the natural world have often been likened to a spider's web, and for good reason. All life on Earth is interconnected in an elegant yet surprisingly simple design, and each living thing is an essential part of that design. To understand biology and the functions of living things, biologists have spent a lot of time looking at the differences among organisms. But in order to understand the very nature of living things, we must first understand what they have in common.

The butterfly larvae and the milkweed—and all animals and plants, for that matter—are made up of the same basic elements. These elements are obtained, used, and eliminated by every living thing in a series of chemical activities called metabolism.

Every molecule of every living tissue must contain carbon. During photosynthesis, green plants take in carbon dioxide from the atmosphere. Within their chlorophyll-filled leaves, in the presence of sunlight, the carbon dioxide is combined with water to form sugar—nature's most basic food. Animals need carbon, too. To grow and function, animals must eat plants or other animals that have fed on plants in order to obtain carbon. When plants and animals die, bacteria and fungi help to break down their tissues. This allows the carbon in plants and animals to be recycled. Indeed, the carbon in your body—and everyone else's body—may once have been inside a dinosaur, a giant redwood, or a monarch butterfly!

All life also needs nitrogen. Nitrogen is an essential component of protoplasm, the complex of chemicals that makes up living cells. Animals acquire nitrogen in the same manner as they acquire carbon dioxide: by eating plants or other animals that have eaten plants. Plants, however, must rely on nitrogen-fixing bacteria in the soil to absorb nitrogen from the atmosphere and convert it into proteins. These proteins are then absorbed from the soil by plant roots.

Living things start life as a single cell. The process by which cells grow and reproduce to become a specific organism—whether the organism is an oak tree or a whale—is controlled by two basic substances called deoxyribonucleic acid (DNA) and ribonucleic acid (RNA). These two chemicals are the building blocks of genes that determine how an organism looks, grows, and functions. Each organism has a unique pattern of DNA and RNA in its genes. This pattern determines all the characteristics of a living thing. Each species passes its unique pattern from generation to generation. Over many billions of years, a process involving genetic mutation and natural selection has allowed species to adapt to a constantly changing environment by evolving—changing genetic patterns. The living creatures we know today are the results of these adaptations.

Reproduction and growth are important to every species, since these are the processes by which new members of a species are created. If a species cannot reproduce and adapt, or if it cannot reproduce fast enough to replace those members that die, it will become extinct (no longer exist).

In recent years, biologists have learned a great deal about how living things function. But there is still much to learn about nature. With high-technology equipment and new information, exciting discoveries are being made every day. New insights and theories quickly make many biology textbooks obsolete. One thing, however, will forever remain certain: As living things, we share an amazing number of characteristics with other forms of life. As animals, our survival depends upon the food and functions provided by other animals and plants. As humans—who can understand the similarities and interdependence among living things—we cannot help but feel connected to the natural world, and we cannot forget our responsibility to protect it. It is only through looking at, and understanding, the rest of the natural world that we can truly appreciate what it means to be "alive."

1

Microorganisms: The Overview

The year was 1675. In Holland, a self-taught scientist named Anton van Leeuwenhoek had become fascinated with making lenses for the simple microscopes in use at the time. One day, he peered through a microscope into a drop taken from a pot of rainwater that had been standing for days. To his astonishment, he saw in the water what he called animalcules ("little animals"). Some of them wiggled and darted around. Others were motionless. Van Leeuwenhoek had discovered a world of life previously unseen.

Microorganisms

The unseen world is the realm of organisms too small to be visible to the human eye, except through a microscope. These extremely tiny life-forms are called microorganisms.

Opposite:
A microphotograph of algae reveals organisms of great beauty. Although most cannot be seen by the naked human eye, microorganisms play many essential roles in the natural world.

Microorganisms behave much as do larger living things that we can see. They compete for food and feed on one another. They contain the basic genetic materials of DNA and other materials needed for reproduction. And they interact in many ways with other living organisms.

Many microorganisms have a number of animal-like characteristics. For almost 300 years, most scientists followed van Leeuwenhoek's theories and considered microorganisms to be members of the animal kingdom. Other microorganisms have plant-like traits—they were thought to belong to the plant kingdom.

Some microorganisms, however, have characteristics of both animals and plants. Scientists have never been certain to which kingdom these belong.

Today, most scientists assign microorganisms to various kingdoms of their own—viewed neither as plants nor animals, but as living things in their own right. Nonetheless, debate continues about the kingdom in which certain species of microorganisms should be placed.

Microorganisms are placed in two kingdoms: the Monera and the Protista. The word *monera* comes from a Greek word meaning "single," referring to single-celled organisms. The most familiar Monera are bacteria (singular, bacterium). Bacteria were among the microorganisms that, until recently, were thought to be plants. Some cause infections that make people ill. Many bacteria, however, are helpful. They help turn milk into yogurt and cheese, aid in the digestion of food, and convert dead animals and plants into soil.

Microorganisms that were previously placed in the animal kingdom are now grouped in Protista. Protozoans form the largest group of protists. The

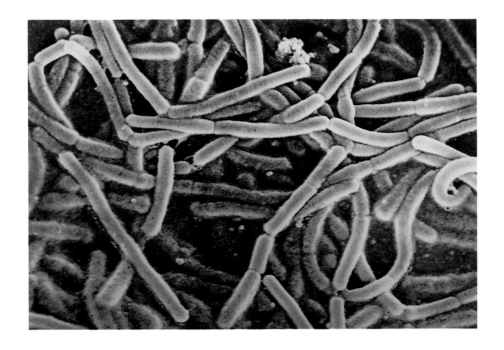

Many bacteria are helpful to humans in the production of foods, beverages, and some medicines. These rod-shaped bacteria, shown here in yogurt, help to ferment milk products.

name *protozoan* comes from Greek words meaning "first animals." Scientists once believed protozoans were the first animals to exist. They were not exactly right. Protozoans do not fit precisely into the definition of an animal, but it is fairly likely that animals developed from them. The most familiar protozoan is probably the amoeba.

Microorganisms are everywhere. Some float in the air, some live in water and soil. They are in food, plants, and the bodies of animals—including you!

Life in a Single Cell

Most bacteria and protozoans are what scientists call unicellular. That means they consist of only one cell. Higher organisms are made of an incredible number of cells. Your body has nerve cells, blood cells, muscle cells, and more—billions of cells of many different types, each type performing a different job. Together, your cells enable you to carry on all the functions that you need to live.

One-celled organisms must carry on many of the same tasks, but all in one cell. Microorganisms have

DID YOU KNOW

Nice Moves

The white blood cells in your body, which attack invading substances such as germs, move in the same way as an amoeba does.

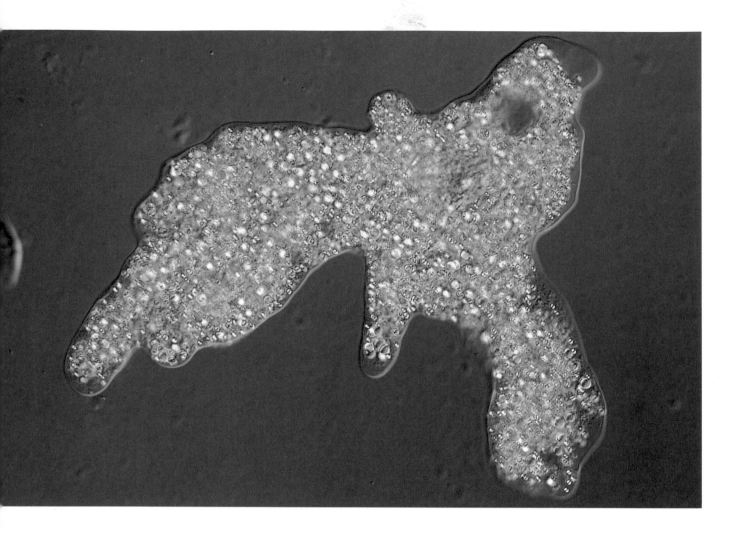

One of the most familiar proto-zoans is the amoeba. Even though they appear to be simple jelly-like masses, amoebas perform all the basic functions of a living organism—including metabolism, reproduction, and reaction to stimuli.

no legs or arms, mouths or eyes, hearts or stomachs. Even so, they must feed, eliminate waste, reproduce, and do everything else that is necessary for survival. Specialized structures within the single cell help perform many of the vital functions accomplished by organs in multicellular organisms. In protozoans, these structures are called organelles. Scientists still do not understand what many of them do or how they manage to do it.

The Good, the Bad, and the Ugly

Microorganisms can be both helpful and harmful to people. Some bacteria cause dangerous diseases, such as staphylococcal infections and some types of pneumonia. Other bacteria, however, are used to

Armored Amoebas

Several relatives of the amoeba, most of which live in the ocean, secrete chalky coverings of lime around their bodies through holes in their shells. When these protozoans die, their shells drop to the ocean bottom. There, they accumulate over vast periods of time, forming limestone and other rocks. Forty-eight million square miles (115 million square kilometers) of ocean floor are covered by the shells of foraminiferans which are a group of "armored" amoebas. The huge pyramids of ancient Egypt were made of rock formed by microscopic foraminiferans that lived millions of years ago. So were the white chalk cliffs of Dover, in England.

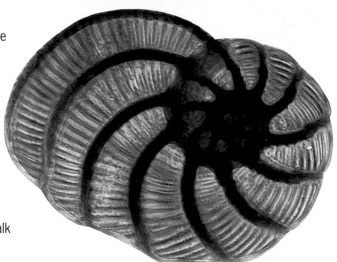

Foraminiferan

make food, including yogurt. Some protozoans also cause diseases, such as malaria and dysentery. On the other hand, microorganisms play an important role in the balance of nature. They furnish food for many tiny animals, which in turn are eaten by larger creatures.

Bacteria Bacteria are believed to be the simplest living organisms, and they were probably the first life-form on Earth. Scientists have identified about 2,000

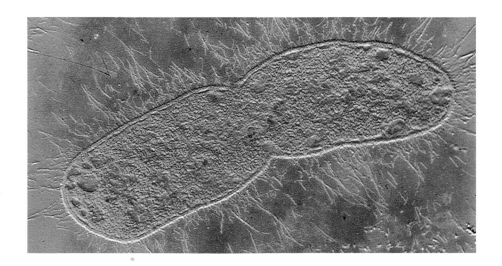

Bacteria, like this *Klebsiella pneumoniae*, are among the smallest living things on Earth.

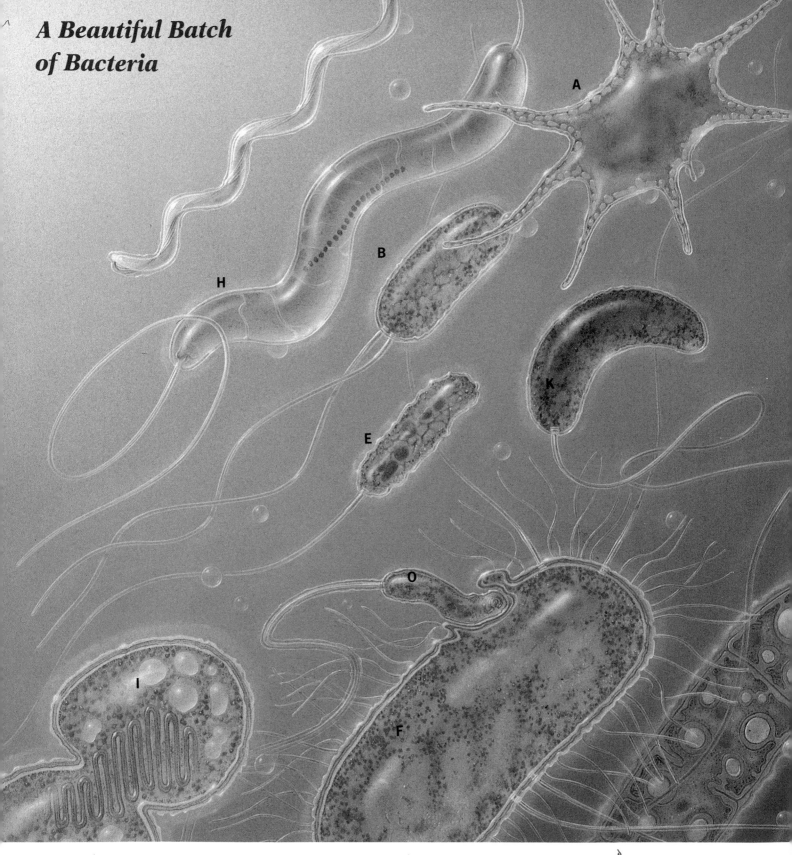

As one of nature's most varied and successful life-forms, bacteria have been able to adapt to almost every environment on Earth—even some without oxygen. The Ancalochloris (**A**), Aquaspirillum (**B**), and Chromatium (**C**) all live in water, where Aquaspirillum can use its magnetically charged particle chain to attract food-rich sediment. Pyrodictium (**D**) thrives in hot habitats, while Rhizobium (**E**) colonizes plant roots and produces a form of nitrogen that helps the plants to survive. Other bacteria, such as Escherichia (**F**), Streptococcus (**G**), and Treponema (**H**) can thrive inside the human body and cause disease. Some bacteria of different types are attracted to one another and, thus, can often be found together in the same environments. Bacteria that can survive in

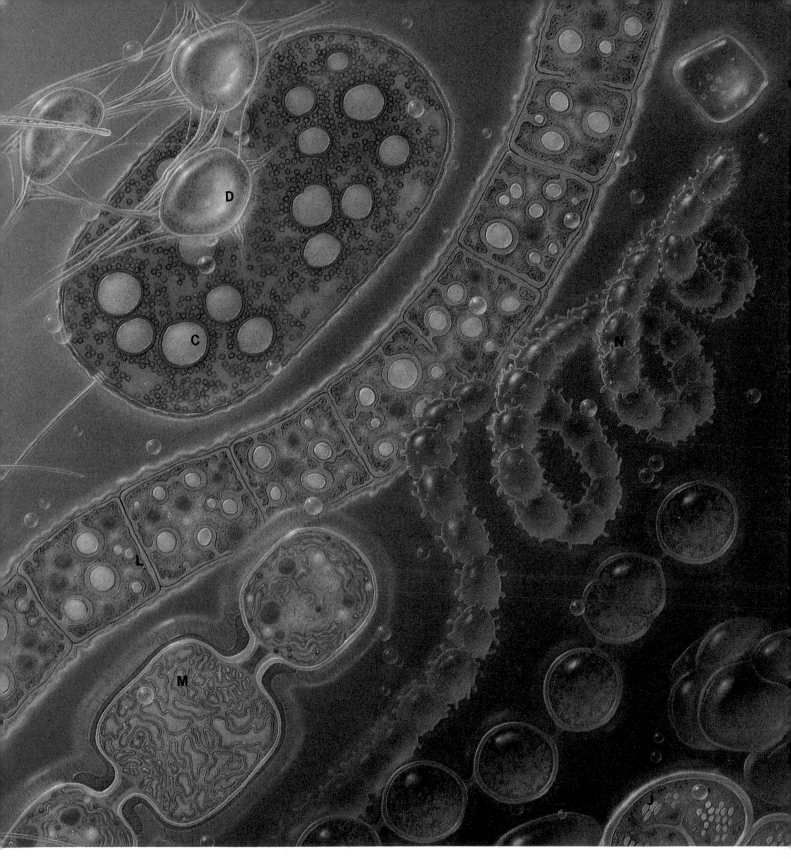

the absence of oxygen (called anaerobic bacteria) sometimes live near other bacteria that produce elements vital to their survival. Methylococcus (**I**), for example, produces methane, which attracts the anaerobic methane consumer Methanosarcina (**J**). Desulfovibrio (**K**) produces hydrogen sulfide and, in turn, attracts Beggiatoa (**L**), which consumes that compound. Other bacteria, such as Anabaena (**M**), produce oxygen from water as they undergo the process of photosynthesis.

Many bacteria are actually helpful to humans in making food and medicine. Streptomyces (**N**), for example, are used in the making of antibiotic medicines and Bdellovibrio (**O**) is valuable because it often attacks many other bacteria.

Simple Anatomy of a Bacterium

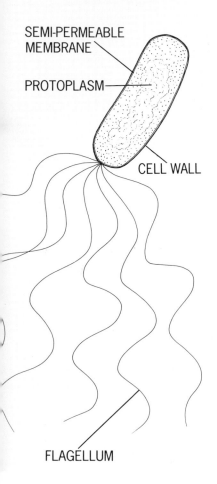

SEMI-PERMEABLE MEMBRANE

PROTOPLASM

CELL WALL

FLAGELLUM

species, or kinds, of bacteria. Some groups of animals, such as insects, have far more species, but in terms of sheer numbers, bacteria are probably the most numerous organisms on Earth. Just a teaspoon of soil may contain many billions of bacteria.

Bacteria are also among the smallest forms of life. An average human weighs 70 trillion times as much as a typical bacterium. Bacteria must be magnified at least 1,000 times to be visible to the naked eye. Large groups, or colonies, of some bacteria can, however, be seen without a microscope.

Scientists who study bacteria grow them in a nutrient mixture called agar, a thick gelatin made from a type of seaweed. A small number of bacteria in agar will quickly multiply into a large colony, sometimes numbering in the billions of inhabitants. Such colonies are visible as small colored spots on the surface of the agar.

There are three main types of bacteria, grouped according to shape. Rod-shaped bacteria are known as bacilli. Round bacteria are called cocci, and those with a roughly spiral shape are called spirilla.

Whatever their shape, all bacteria have a hard wall made of cellulose, a compound of sugar molecules. The outside of the cell wall is usually coated with a layer of slimy material. The hard cell wall provides support, like the bones of the human skeleton and the stiff cell walls of plants. The presence of a stiff cell wall in bacteria is why scientists once thought of them as simple plants.

Lining the inside of a bacterium's cell wall is a flexible cell membrane. It acts as a protective skin over the bulk of the living matter within the cell called protoplasm. All living cells, including those of plants and animals, are made up of protoplasm and are protected by a cell membrane. Food and oxygen pass

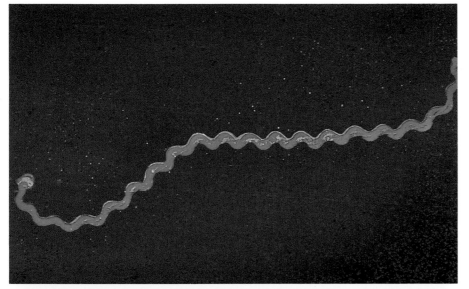

The Three Kinds of Bacteria

Bacteria are grouped according to their shape into three main categories. The roughly shaped spiral bacteria, such as this leptospira (*top*), is from the family spirilla. Rod-shaped bacteria, like this proteus (*middle*), are known as bacilli. Round-shaped bacteria, such as the *Neisseria meningitidis* (*bottom*), are called cocci.

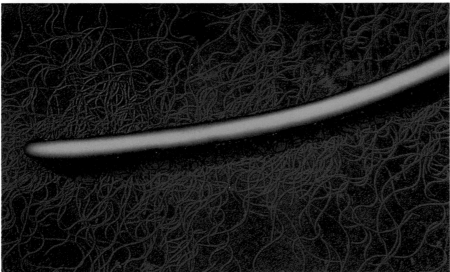

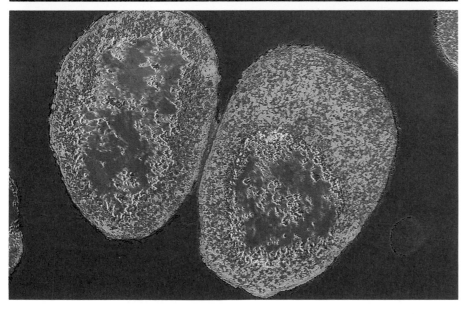

through the membrane into the cell, and wastes pass out. Unlike the cells of protozoans, plants, and animals, however, the bacterial cell lacks a nucleus—the control center that regulates a cell's activities.

Most bacteria cannot move on their own. Instead, they are carried by the wind and water and on other living things. Some bacteria can move on their own through liquid, swimming with the aid of a tail-like structure, called a flagellum. Some species have only one such structure, others have several.

Protozoans Scientists differ on the exact number of protozoan species that exist. It may be about 30,000 or as high as 80,000. Certainly, many have never been identified. Most of them live in water or other moist habitats, such as mud. Protozoans can be found in oceans, ponds, lakes, streams, and other bodies of water around the world. They also inhabit soil. Some live inside the bodies of animals.

The cell of a protozoan resembles the cells that, all together, make up your own body. A cell membrane encloses the protozoan's cytoplasm, the protoplasm surrounding a nucleus. The nucleus is the cell's "brain"—it directs the cell's activities.

The Blue-Green Scene

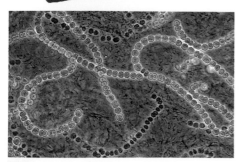
Blue-green algae

Besides bacteria, another group of monera is the blue-green algae. (Not all are bluish green: in fact, some are red.) Blue-green algae are very close to plants, although some of them can move. They contain chlorophyll, the material that gives plants their green color. Like plants, blue-green algae use chlorophyll to capture the energy of sunlight for food.

Blue-green algae are found in a wide variety of environments, including hot springs, deserts, glaciers, and ponds. Large numbers of these algae sometimes coat a lake or pond with a green to blue-green layer.

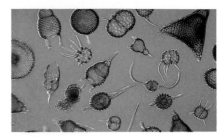
The variety of protozoans Like all living things, protozoans are divided by scientists into groups. The amoebas belong to a class known as the sarcodina. An amoeba resembles a tiny blob of jelly that changes shape within its cell membrane. When an amoeba wants to move, it extends a projection of its cell membrane in the direction of travel. Cytoplasm flows into the projection, which is called a pseudopod, or "false foot." (The pseudopod is an organelle.) Cytoplasm behind the pseudopod continues to flow into it, and the membrane stretches to contain it until the amoeba is reformed in a new location. In this way, the amoeba just keeps oozing along, but not very fast. An amoeba can spend several days traveling and move only a few inches.

Another group of protists are the flagellates, named for the long, whip-like appendage, or flagellum, that they swing back and forth in order to swim. (The flagellum is an organelle.) Still another group of protozoans are the ciliates. Their

Principal Features of an Amoeba

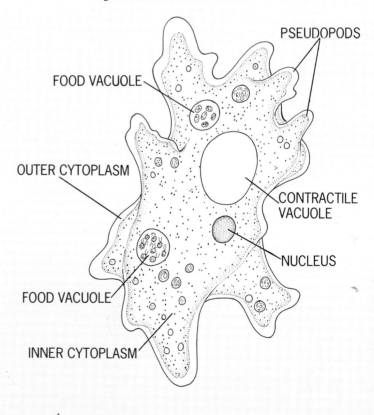

PSEUDOPODS

FOOD VACUOLE

OUTER CYTOPLASM

CONTRACTILE VACUOLE

NUCLEUS

FOOD VACUOLE

INNER CYTOPLASM

The In-Between-a Euglena

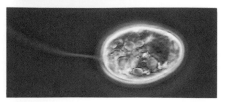

Euglena

The euglena is a flagellate that uses chlorophyll, like plants, to make food. But it moves rapidly and behaves like many protozoans. Some scientists have considered the euglena as algae. Most, however, group it in the Kingdom Protista. Either way, the euglena is an in-between organism, with some traits of simple plants and some of simple animals. The euglena travels by whipping its flagellum back and forth, which sends it hurtling through the water like a football spiraling through the air.

name comes from the tiny hair-like projections on the cell membrane that are used to move the creature through the water. (Cilia are also organelles.)

Yet another group of protozoans are the sporozoans. Most cannot move on their own, at least as adults. During reproduction (the process by which organisms produce new individuals of their own species) sporozoans develop into thick-walled cells, called spores.

Sporozoans live in the bodies of animals. They are parasites, which means they feed on cells and other materials of the animals they infest. One

The euglena is a kind of protist known as a flagellate. Flagellates are named for their long, tail-like appendages, which whip back and forth in order to propel the organism forward.

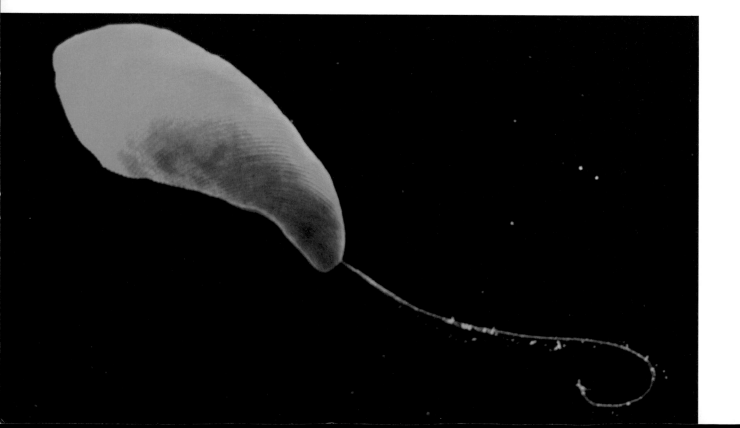

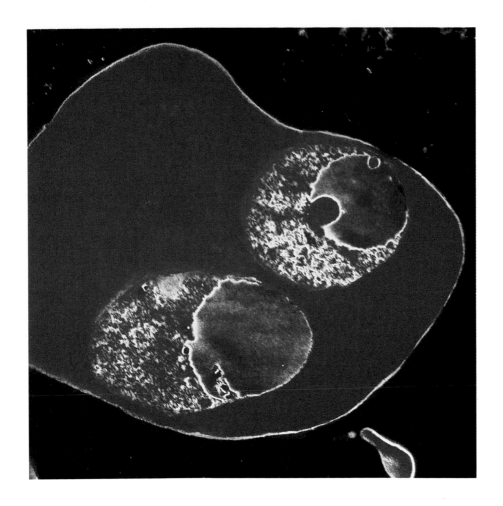

Two plasmodium sporozoites invade a human red blood cell. Sporozoans are parasites that feed on the living cells of animals they infest.

sporozoan causes the disease malaria. Its spores are transmitted from one infected person or animal to another by certain mosquitoes. The spores enter female mosquitoes when they withdraw blood from infected people or other animals. Inside the mosquitoes, the spores develop and move to the glands that produce saliva. When the mosquito bites someone else, the malaria protozoans are transmitted.

Despite their tiny size, all these microorganisms carry on complex, life-sustaining activities. Many of their functions and life processes are in certain ways very similar to those of humans and other living things. As the following pages show, reaction to stimuli, metabolism, reproduction, and growth all take place even on the tiniest levels of this wondrous and fascinating unseen world.

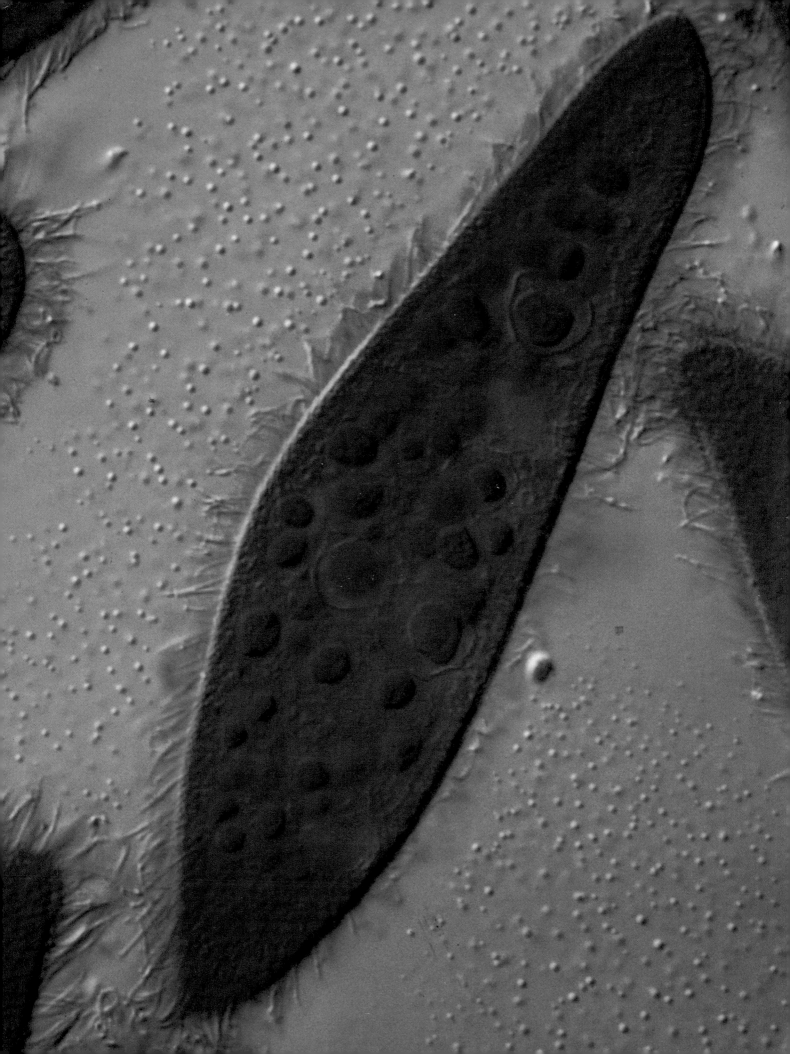

2

How Microorganisms React

 Whether it is an amoeba in a drop of water or an elephant on the African savannah, living things react to the changes in their surroundings. Change that causes a reaction, or response, in a living organism is called a stimulus (plural, stimuli). Organisms are bombarded with stimuli every moment of their lives. All together, the reactions of an organism to stimuli make up an organism's behavior.

Animals receive stimuli with their sense organs, such as eyes, ears, taste buds, and nerve cells sensitive to touch. Microorganisms do not have sense organs. They cannot see, hear, taste, or smell. Still, many react to certain stimuli, although in ways different from those of higher organisms.

Scientists know very little about the reactions of microorganisms. This is especially true of bacteria. In fact, the majority of bacteria, which lack the power of motion, may not react to stimuli at all. Some mobile bacteria, however, do seem to react to certain

Opposite:
Like all living things, microorganisms must react effectively to their surroundings in order to survive. This paramecium has an exterior coating of hairs called cilia that seem to sense stimuli and also help the organism to move.

That's Touching

Some parts of the paramecium's body seem more sensitive to touch than others. Experiments show that a light touch to the rear of a paramecium's body sends it scurrying away. The same intensity of touch elsewhere, however, does not cause a reaction.

chemicals. For instance, they seem to home in on certain nutrients, which they eat. It may be, however, that such movements are random: that is, they do not follow any purposeful pattern and are not a direct response to stimuli.

Protozoans are a different story. Some of them respond in definite ways to specific stimuli. Just as in higher organisms, the reactions of protozoans to stimuli help them survive. Basically, the behavior of microorganisms involves feeding, getting away from danger, and reproducing. A protozoan either moves toward or away from a stimulus. The behavior of single-celled organisms is not conscious, however, since microorganisms have no brains. They exist, but do not know it.

Touch

Most protozoans are sensitive to touch, or contact with other objects in their surroundings. In fact, touch is probably responsible for more behavior by protozoans than any other kind of stimulus. The main functions of touch seem to be to get food and to avoid becoming the food of something else.

Amoebas have been studied more extensively by scientists than most other protozoans. Many experiments have shown how an amoeba reacts to touch. Amoebas first sense the touch of an object with the cell membrane, then with all their protoplasm. When an amoeba is touched with a tiny glass rod, it may try to flow around it or turn aside.

The paramecium is another commonly studied protozoan. If a rapidly swimming paramecium bangs into another object, it will quickly move away from it. But if the paramecium has been traveling slowly, it may remain with the object. This behavior may be related to feeding. Ciliates, such as the paramecium, seem to sense objects with some of their cilia. Flagellates, such as the euglena, may use their whip-like organelle to sense touch.

Light

Some protozoans also react to changes in light. In nature, an amoeba experiences the same routine of gradual brightening and dimming of daylight during each 24-hour period. Amoebas do not appear to react to such gradual changes in light. But if an amoeba in a laboratory suddenly encounters a bright light, it will quickly pull away. If an amoeba traveling in one direction repeatedly meets a bright light, it will eventually change direction.

The euglena reacts strongly to light. Near the flagellum of the euglena is a red dot, called an eyespot, that is sensitive to light. Euglenas gather around a strong source of light. In darkness, they spread out. Their attraction to light, as we will see in the next chapter, helps them obtain food.

Chemicals

Amoebas are also sensitive to certain chemicals. An amoeba that touches a drop of salt solution will quickly pull back. Parameciums also stay away from salt solution, a fact proven in many experiments.

When a paramecium encounters a disagreeable chemical stimulus, it reverses the motion of its cilia and backs up. Then the paramecium tries to work around the area where the chemical is located. As it moves, the paramecium tests the water for the chemical. It does this with a channel-like indentation in its surface, called the oral groove. The groove is lined with cilia that draw in water as they beat. When the paramecium no longer detects the chemical in the water, it continues its forward movement.

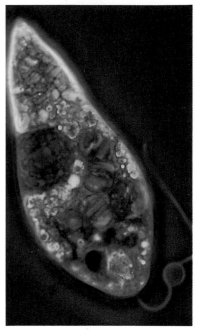

The euglena reacts strongly to light stimuli. A light-sensitive eyespot near the flagellum enables it to sense changes in light levels and to adapt its behavior accordingly.

A paramecium can constantly test its surroundings for chemicals by using a channel-like indentation in its side called an oral groove.

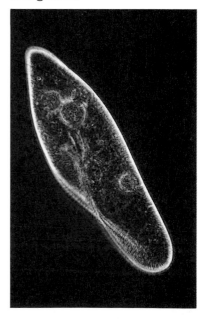

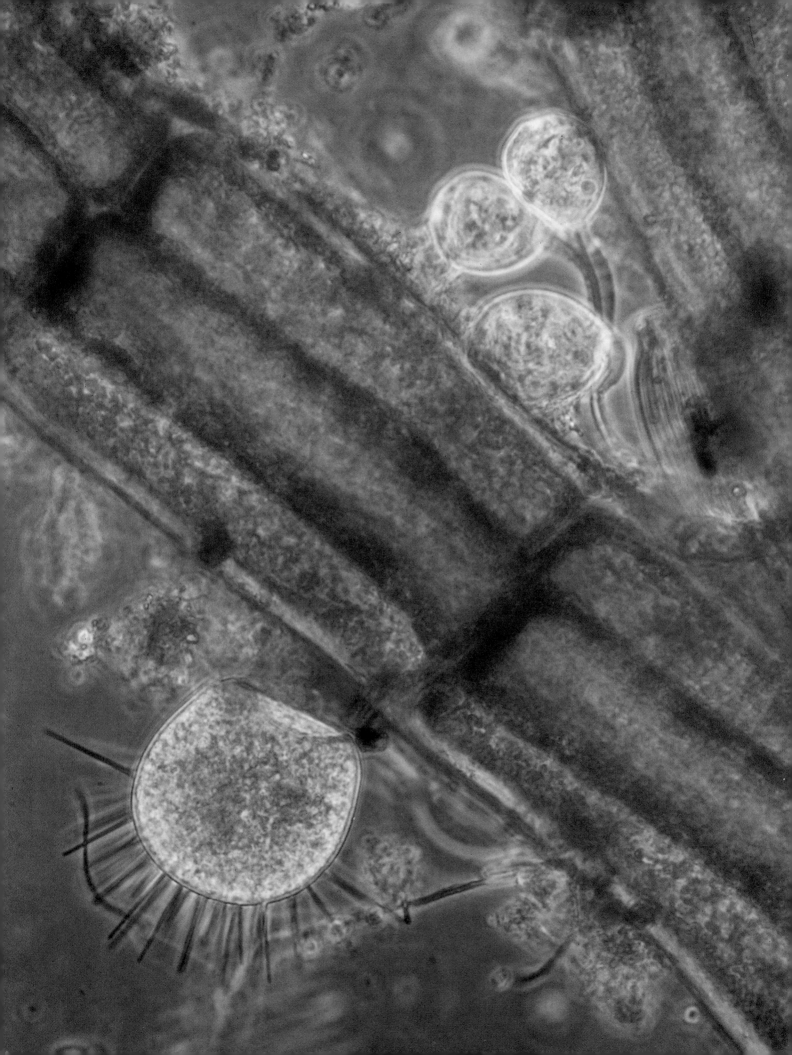

3

How Microorganisms Function

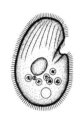 All living things need energy to grow and function. Your body breaks down food into chemicals that can be further broken down by your cells. The cells combine these chemicals with oxygen to produce energy.

Getting food, storing it, and then converting it to energy involve chemical processes that keep organisms alive. So too does the elimination of wastes. Together, all these processes are called metabolism.

Metabolism Basics

The basics of metabolism are fairly simple. An organism needs to obtain food. Once food is eaten, it is broken down—in an animal's body it is done in the mouth, stomach, and small intestine, by digestion. Meanwhile, oxygen enters when the animal breathes. When the oxygen combines with food in cells, energy is released. Oxygen also triggers the release of energy

Opposite:
Suctorians are protozoans that use their tentacles to paralyze their prey. Here, a round suctorean hangs from some algae. Microorganisms, like all living things, need food for energy in order to survive.

These three sequential photographs show how an amoeba surrounds its prey before ingesting it. An amoeba's pseudopods will sense nearby food and then encircle it in order to trap it in a food vacuole for digestion.

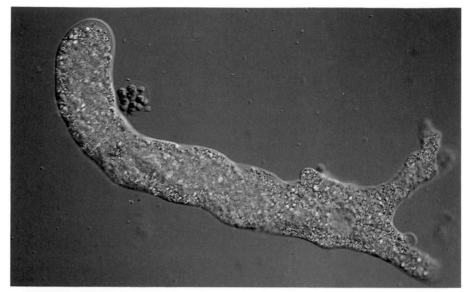

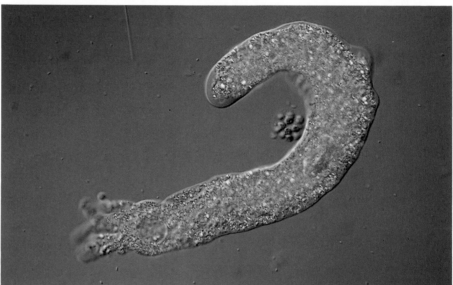

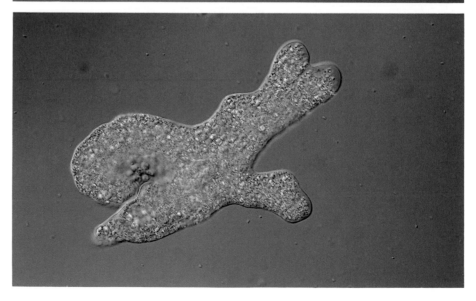

from many other substances. Oxygen is needed for wood to burn. Burning wood releases both light and heat energy.

Ash is a waste product of wood, remaining after the flammable material has been used. Two products of animal metabolism are water and carbon dioxide. In humans and many other animals, water leaves as urine, and carbon dioxide leaves when the animal exhales. Other waste products, such as undigested matter, are eliminated as solid waste, or feces.

Since a microorganism has no digestive organs, obtaining and breaking down nutrients is carried out by different processes than in animals. But the basics and results of metabolism are the same—and the whole process begins with getting food.

How Protozoans Eat

Protozoans eat one another, bacteria, algae, and tiny animals. They get food in many ways. Some sweep in food with their cilia or flagella from the water or other fluid environments. Other protozoans suck their food in. Still others engulf it. As in the case of a person or an ant, the aim is to bring food within the body—or in the case of a protozoan, to bring it within the cell.

The blob An amoeba literally surrounds its food, flowing like a blob around its prey. As an amoeba moves about in search of something to eat, sooner or later one of its pseudopods will touch an edible organism. Once this happens, the pseudopod will encircle it along with a droplet of the water in which it was floating. Trapped within the amoeba, this water droplet becomes an organelle called a food vacuole. There, the food is digested. An amoeba can eat hundreds of other protozoans, such as parameciums, in a single day.

How an Amoeba Eats

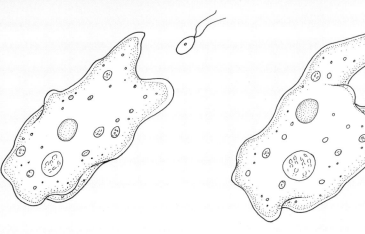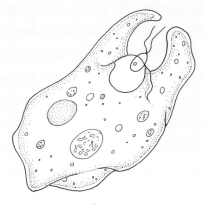

A.
The amoeba moves
toward an organism.

B.
Pseudopods begin
to extend.

C.
The pseudopods encircle the
organism, and a thin layer of
cytoplasm covers its top.

DID YOU KNOW

The Digestion Question

Bacteria do not digest food
internally. They get energy
from chemical reactions in their
surroundings. Instead of
breaking down compounds
within their bodies, they do it
outside, with chemicals that they
produce. In effect, bacteria
excrete chemicals that digest
parts of their environment. Most
animals, on the other hand,
break down food chemically
inside their bodies. The energy
they need is produced internally.

Filter feeders A paramecium is an example of a filter feeder. During feeding, it shoots out threads from between its cilia. The threads are sticky and anchor the paramecium in place while it filters food from the water.

A paramecium moves its cilia to churn up the water into currents. The currents bring food—such as smaller protozoans and bacteria—into its oral groove, which works almost like a mouth. At the end of the indentation is a tube in which the food gathers. From there, it enters water-filled food vacuoles for digestion.

How Protozoans Digest

Protozoans digest internally, with enzymes similar to those that animals use to break down food. The enzymes are produced within a protozoan's cell. Through the microscope, one can actually see digestion at work within a protozoan. The food particle actually grows in size, while its shape becomes fuzzy. Then it becomes transparent, shrinks, and finally disappears as the protozoan cell digests and absorbs

28

How Microorganisms Function

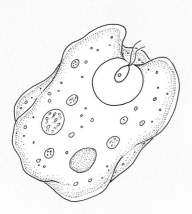
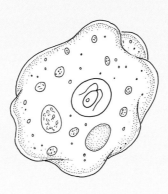
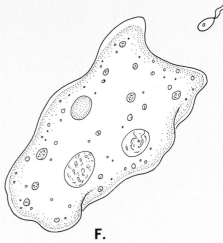

D.
A thin layer of cytoplasm covers the bottom of the organism, now almost completely enclosed.

E.
The organism lies in the amoeba's cytoplasm, inside a food vacuole.

F.
The organism is digested as the amoeba begins to hunt again.

it. The broken-down food then becomes part of the protoplasm of the cell, just as it does in cells of your own body. A protozoan uses the nutrients from its food for immediate energy or stores it for later use.

The waste that remains includes carbon dioxide, water, and a chemical called urea, a compound that contains nitrogen and is found in urine. Most protozoans excrete waste through their cell membranes. After an amoeba digests food, for example, tiny vacuoles form around its wastes and excess water. These vacuoles gather together and form a larger one, called a contractile vacuole. It then moves to the outer rim of the cell and spits out the waste and water, which burst through

Anatomy of a Paramecium

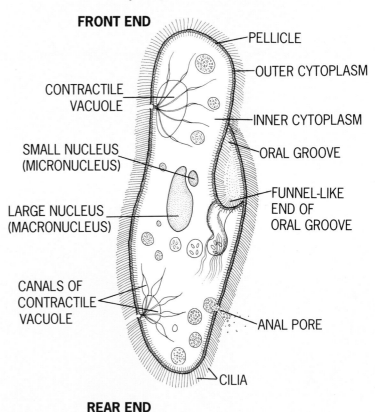

FRONT END

PELLICLE

OUTER CYTOPLASM

CONTRACTILE VACUOLE

INNER CYTOPLASM

SMALL NUCLEUS (MICRONUCLEUS)

ORAL GROOVE

LARGE NUCLEUS (MACRONUCLEUS)

FUNNEL-LIKE END OF ORAL GROOVE

CANALS OF CONTRACTILE VACUOLE

ANAL PORE

CILIA

REAR END

the membrane. Once the wastes are excreted, the membrane recloses. A paramecium expels waste somewhat differently, sending it through pores in the membrane.

How Protozoans Get Oxygen

Protozoans eliminate their carbon dioxide waste by passing it through the cell membrane. Oxygen, which the cell needs to make energy, enters the cell the same way. Protozoans can get oxygen directly from their surroundings. When the cell of an amoeba releases carbon dioxide and obtains oxygen, it is functioning in a way similar to a blood cell in a fish's gills.

Bacteria live in many things humans eat or use and, given the proper conditions and enough time, they will begin to break down those materials in which they live. The brown rot on this apple was caused first by bacteria that began to feed on the fruit; then by a mold that invaded to feed on and decompose the apple.

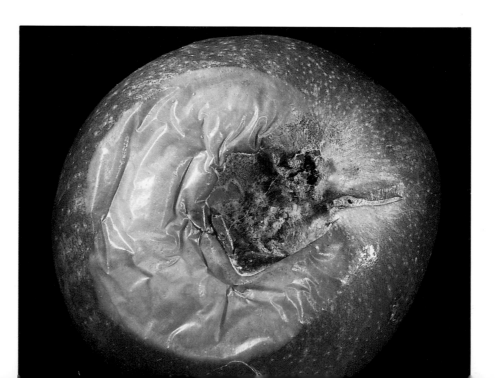

What Bacteria Eat

Bacteria live in and on all sorts of things: every kind of food we eat, wood, paper, oil—you name it. Brown rot on an apple is evidence that bacteria are eating it. Feeding by bacteria turns milk sour. Some feed on the chemicals in petroleum, so they are used to clean up oil spills. Others are able to take energy from inorganic (nonliving) matter.

Two Ways to Feed

Scientists put bacteria into two groups, according to how they get their food. Those that break down chemicals of inorganic matter for energy are called autotrophs. Those that feed on organic matter are heterotrophs—most bacteria are heterotrophs.

Autotrophs A few autotrophs contain chlorophyll, just like plants. Just as plants do, they use it to make food by the process called photosynthesis. In the presence of sunlight, the bacteria combine carbon dioxide and water to make their food. Other autotrophs create food from chemical reactions that involve nitrogen, iron, and sulfur. The sulfurous smell from rotten eggs is caused by bacteria.

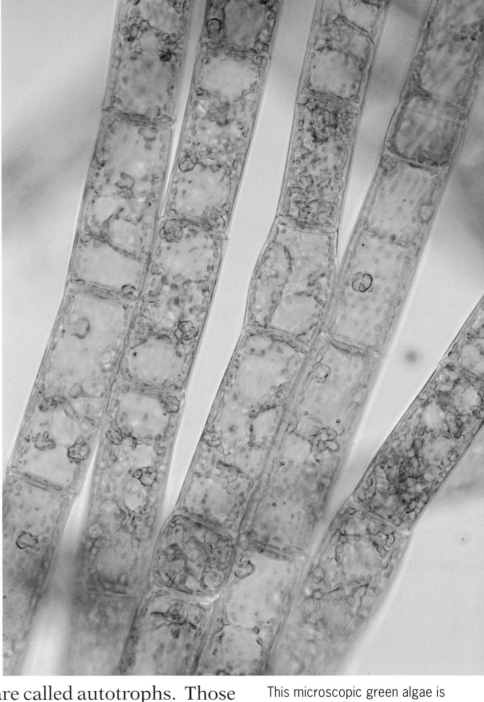

This microscopic green algae is an example of an autotroph. It uses its chlorophyll to makes its own food through the process of photosynthesis.

Mini-Monsters

Suctorians are protozoans that cannot move once they become adults. Even so, they can catch other protozoans to eat. The suctorian has long tentacles with a multipurpose knob on the end of each. The knobs paralyze organisms. Once the prey is paralyzed, the suctorian sucks the prey's cytoplasm through its knobs and down the tentacles into the main part of the cell, where it is digested.

Another mini-monster is the didinium. This fierce hunter, who especially seeks out the paramecium, is much smaller than its prey. But it makes no difference. Didinium extends a tube that attaches to the paramecium and seems to paralyze it. Then the didinium stretches and slides over the paramecium, rather like a sock over a foot. After that, the didinium absorbs its meal.

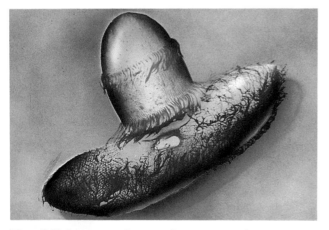

The didinium attaches to the paramecium and paralyzes it.

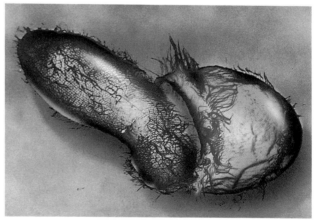

The didinium begins to stretch itself over its prey.

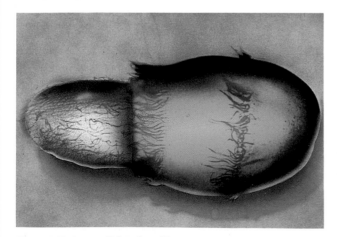

The didinium slides itself over the paramecium as it stretches.

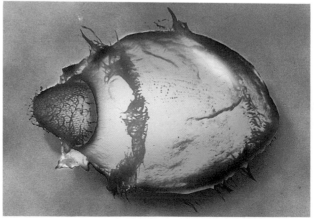

The paramecium is almost completely engulfed.

Heterotrophs Heterotrophs live on organic matter in their surroundings. When heterotrophic bacteria attack an apple, for instance, they secrete chemicals called enzymes—the same kinds of chemicals that also play a part in animal digestion. The enzymes digest nutrients in the apple and convert them to chemicals that are gradually absorbed by the bacteria.

Some heterotrophs feed on dead organic matter. In order to do this, some of them break down dead vegetation and animals into materials that form soil. This process is called decay and is essential to the life and growth of plants and—by relation—all animals. Tooth decay is another form of decay. It is caused in large part by bacteria breaking down food particles that are left on teeth.

Other heterotrophs get their nourishment from live organisms. They attack living cells and tissues, and many of them can cause disease.

Some Bacteria Can Live Without Oxygen (Gasp!)

Most bacteria also absorb oxygen. But some do not and, in fact, cannot function in oxygen. This type is called anaerobic bacteria. The bacteria in the soil that fix nitrogen are anaerobic bacteria. In the presence of oxygen, anaerobic bacteria break apart. They do not necessarily die, however. Instead, a thick coat forms around a bacterium's DNA and other parts necessary for life, forming what is called an endospore. The endospore cannot perform life functions. As long as a bacterium is in the presence of oxygen, it remains an endospore. Thus protected, it may stay in this inactive state for many years, until livable conditions return. At that point, it becomes an active bacterium once more.

The Light Side

A euglena is its own food factory. It makes food like a green plant, using the energy of sunlight to combine carbon dioxide gas and water into sugars for food. It is not surprising, therefore, that a euglena is attracted to light, just like a green plant.

Toil in the Soil

If you have a garden, you may know that fertilizer with nitrogen makes green beans and other plants grow better. Plants need nitrogen, but they cannot get it from the air. Certain bacteria that live in the soil take nitrogen from the air and use it for energy. As they do, they "fix" nitrogen in the soil in a form plants can use. These nitrogen-fixing bacteria are essential for plant growth, and thus, essential for human life on our planet.

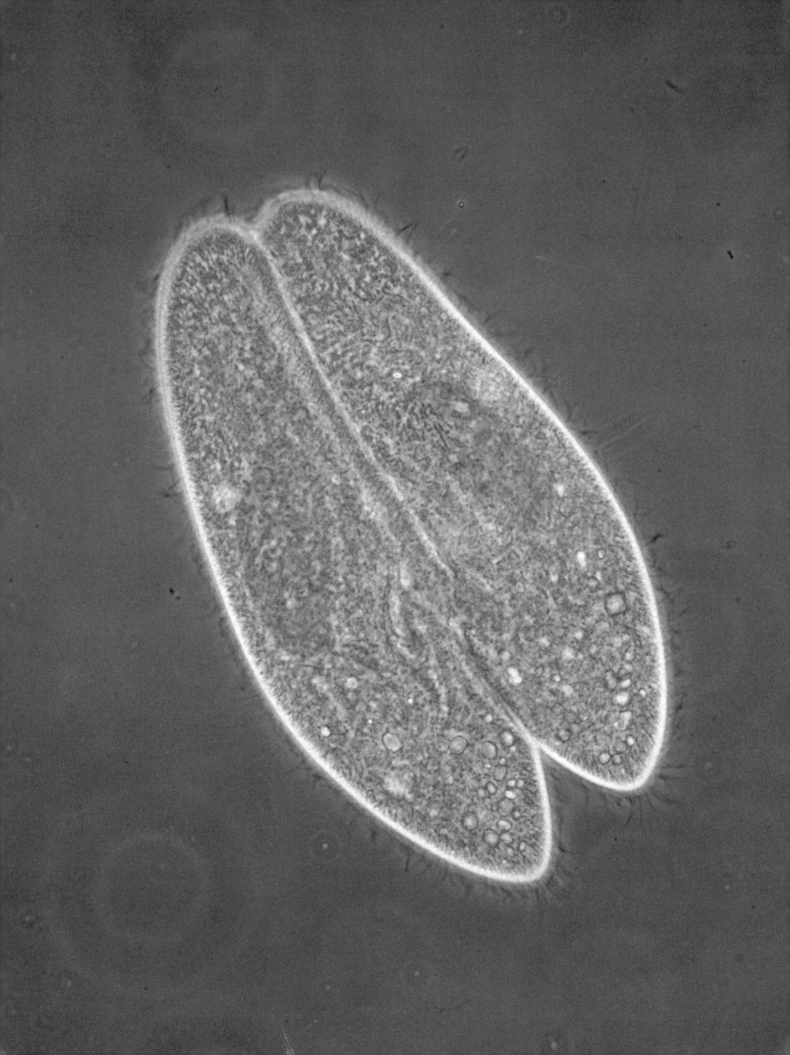

4

Reproduction and Growth

In a pond, an amoeba eats and eats until it grows fat. After a while, its cell takes the shape of a ball. Then it lengthens. About halfway down its length, the cell begins to constrict. It pinches inward until it looks as if it has a waist. The "waist" becomes smaller and smaller until the cell breaks in two. Has the amoeba self-destructed? Not at all. It has formed two new amoebas, each identical to the other and to the cell from which they were formed. The original amoeba has produced two new members of its own species. This process is called reproduction.

Reproduction keeps a species in existence. In order to survive, a species must be able to produce enough new individuals to replace those that die. Otherwise, the species will become extinct. This is true for all living things, from bacteria to human beings.

Opposite:
Two parameciums are joined together at their oral grooves during the process of reproduction. Creating more members of a species is one of the most important functions of any living organism.

Two Kinds of Reproduction

Many living things reproduce by joining a male sex cell with a female sex cell. The male sex cell is commonly known as a sperm; the female, an ovum, or egg. The cell that forms when the two join is called a zygote. This form of creating new individuals is called sexual reproduction.

Some simple organisms are able to reproduce in a different way. Like an amoeba, one individual can produce others, all on its own. The term for this method is asexual reproduction. Asexual reproduction has certain advantages. It is fast, and the new cells are exact, but smaller, replicas of the original organism. The young also do not have to spend time developing.

Bacteria and protozoans reproduce asexually. Some protozoans, however, can reproduce through

Divide and Conquer: How an Amoeba Reproduces

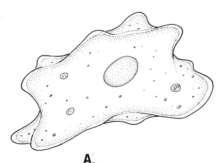

A.
Amoeba before division.

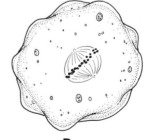

B.
Amoeba becomes round as nucleus begins first stages of division.

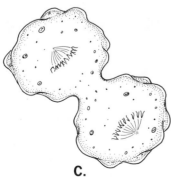

C.
Nucleus and cytoplasm both divide.

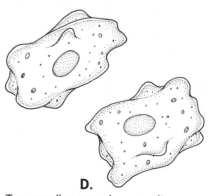

D.
Two smaller amoebas result, each with a nucleus and half the cytoplasm of the original.

Let's Split

Binary means two. Fission means to break up. Binary fission is a method of asexual reproduction in which—as in the amoeba—one organism splits into two. Binary fission happens all the time in your body. The multiplication of cells causes growth and the healing of injuries, such as cuts.

During binary fission, DNA—the chemical that transfers genetic characteristics—from the original cell goes to both of its "daughter" cells. That DNA transfers the characteristics of the original to its offspring. As an amoeba splits through binary fission, its cell nucleus, which contains DNA, divides in two. Each of the new amoebas gets its own part of the divided nucleus. An amoeba can become two new amoebas in about an hour, from the start to the finish of binary fission.

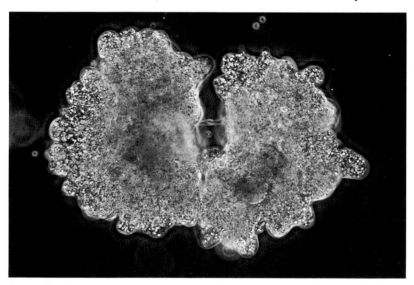

Amoeba during binary fission

the union of two individuals. There are no sexes among protozoans, but the process still resembles a form of sexual reproduction.

How the euglena splits Many protozoans also reproduce by binary fission. The euglena is one example. After the nucleus divides, the euglena's organelles, such as the eyespot and flagellum, are reproduced in the rear of the cell. When the euglena splits, each daughter cell then has a complete set of organelles.

A euglena may cover itself with a hard shell called a cyst, and can reproduce within it. In this form of reproduction, the euglena divides lengthwise. Sometimes, there may be several divisions of euglena cells before the cyst disappears and sets them free.

The paramecium reproduces two ways A paramecium is another protozoan that can reproduce by binary fission. But splitting up is complicated for a paramecium. A paramecium has two nuclei, one bigger than the other. The larger is the macronucleus, which controls most functions of the paramecium cell. The smaller, the micronucleus, contains DNA and controls reproduction.

When a paramecium divides, the micronucleus splits and the two halves move to opposite ends of the cell. The macronucleus divides lengthwise. New organelles develop at each end of the cell. Then the paramecium itself divides down the middle.

It takes a paramecium about two hours to divide itself. When conditions are right, a paramecium can divide two or three times in a day.

Conjugation Parameciums can also reproduce in a way that is commonly considered a form of sexual reproduction because it involves the joining of two separate organisms.

Reproduction by a pair of parameciums is called conjugation, which comes from Latin words that mean "joining together." It is somewhat similar to the conjugation by which one bacterium transfers DNA to another. Conjugation by bacteria is not reproduction, however, because it does not create new individuals.

Conjugation requires two different mating types of paramecium with differing DNA. These two types are not really two different sexes, but they serve the same purpose.

Bacteria Hysteria

Like an amoeba, bacteria also reproduce by binary fission. Their rate of reproduction is amazing. Some bacteria undergo binary fission every 20 minutes. That means that in 20 minutes, one bacterium will become two. Twenty minutes later, there will be four. In another 20 minutes, eight bacteria will be present. At that rate, within seven hours there could be more than 2 million of them! Bacteria will not reproduce at cold temperatures—which is why milk keeps longer in the refrigerator than out in the sun. In warmer temperatures, however, the bacteria in milk grow rapidly, turning it sour.

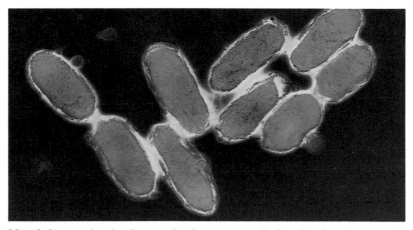

Yersinia pestis, the bacteria that causes bubonic plague

When a paramecium is ready to conjugate, it gets sticky. This stickiness allows it to join with another paramecium at the surface of its oral groove. As in bacteria, a bridge of protoplasm forms between the pair, which continue to swim.

The macronucleus of each paramecium breaks down and disappears, and the micronucleus divides. Now each paramecium has two nuclei, which, in turn, divide again, leaving four nuclei in each member of the paramecium pair. Then, three of each four nuclei disappear and the one remaining divides into two parts, one larger than the other. Next, the pair of parameciums exchange the small nuclei through the protoplasm bridge.

Within each paramecium, the exchanged nucleus joins the one already there, similar to the way a male sperm and female egg form a zygote. Then the pair of parameciums separates. But the process of reproduction is still not over.

Each new zygote multiplies into eight. Four enlarge into macronuclei; three others disappear; and one remains a micronucleus. Then each paramecium divides. Thus far, the process has made two cells into four, but it is still not over. Again, each paramecium divides, bringing the total to eight, each with one micronucleus and one macronucleus.

Volvox reproduction Volvox is a green protozoan, like a euglena. The volvox reproduces in an

A volvox is a protozoan that reproduces in two stages. The first stage, in which masses of cells undergo binary fission, is asexual. The second stage, in which the cells develop into males and females, is a form of sexual reproduction.

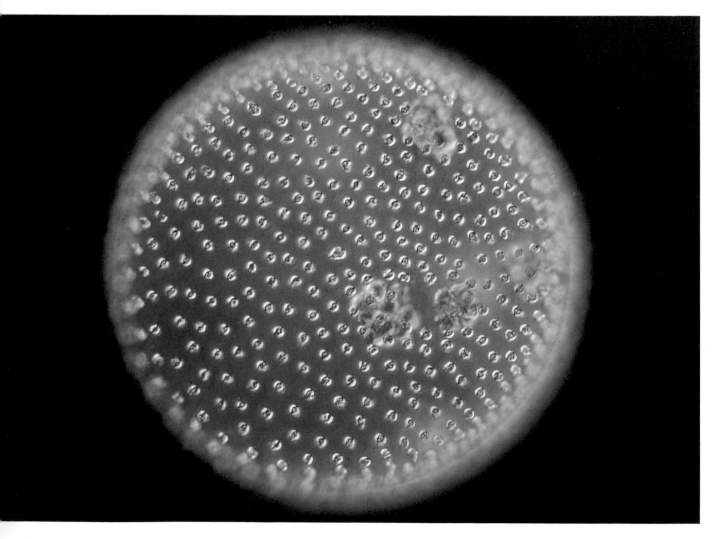

Paramecium Division

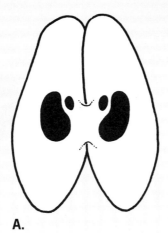

A.

Two parameciums unite
by their oral grooves.

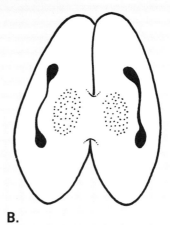

B.

In each paramecium, the large
nucleus begins to disintegrate.
Then the small nucleus begins
to divide.

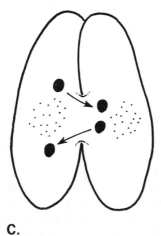

C.

One of the two small nuclei in
each paramecium migrates to
the partner.

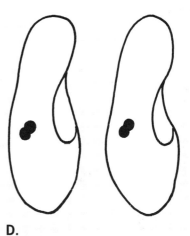

D.

In each paramecium, the two
small nuclei fuse into a new
nucleus. Then the parameciums
separate.

E.

In each paramecium, the new
small nucleus divides several
times, eventually giving rise to
both large and small nuclei.

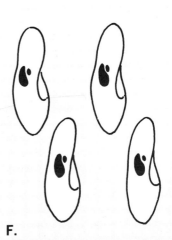

F.

Each paramecium then divides
twice, resulting in four small parameciums.

amazing two-step process—the first step asexual, the second sexual.

This protozoan lives in a colony composed of thousands of cells. The colony is shaped like a ball and is hollow and watery inside. Its walls are composed of thousands of cells linked by threads of protoplasm, and with tail-like organelles, similar to a euglena's. The "tails" beat continuously, rolling the ball through the water.

At the start of reproduction, a small number of cells lose their "tails" and form hollow masses within the colony, the rest of which disintegrates. The

A volvox with a colony of recently formed zygotes inside. These zygotes are a product of the second—or sexual—phase of volvox reproduction.

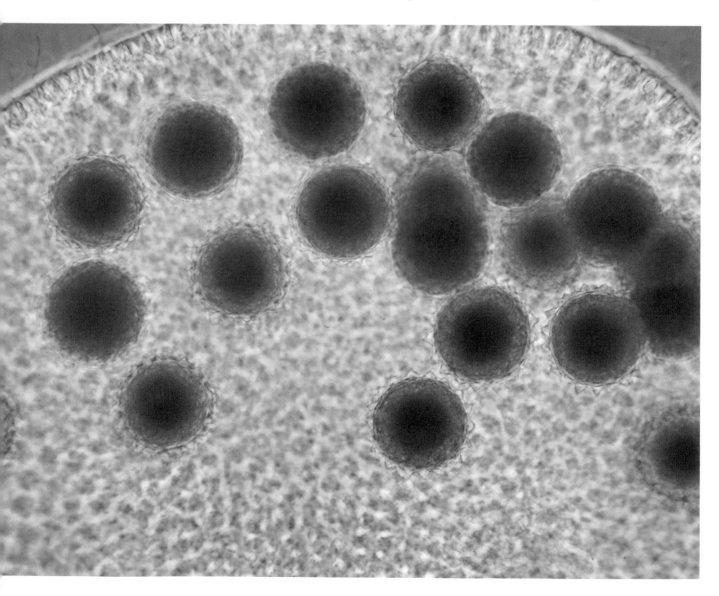

Quick Change

For a species to survive, it must adapt to changes in its environment. Adaptations take many forms, including senses, shapes, and behavior. A species does not adapt on purpose. It happens by chance, over many generations. If an adaptation happens to suit a key environmental change, the species has an advantage.

Adaptation also causes variation in a species. The more varied its individuals, the better chance the species has of surviving. For example, if a species of mammal has some members with short hair and others with long hair, the species as a whole has a better chance of surviving changes in climate. A cool climate would favor long-haired individuals, a warm climate would better suit those with short hair. One type or the other might disappear, but the species itself would survive.

Species of bacteria have the ability to undergo variation in a very short time—and they do it in several ways. Some species have the ability to transfer DNA between the individuals. This is done by the process called conjugation.

The species that undergo conjugation include individuals of two types—those that contain DNA material called plasmids and those that do not. Two individuals, one of each type, build a bridge of cytoplasm between them. Then the bacterium with plasmids passes one of them to the bacterium facing it. That means the recipient now can pass the plasmid—and whatever genetic characteristics it contains—to its descendants. They will have new characteristics that would not have occurred without conjugation.

This sort of variation creates problems in the treatment of diseases caused by bacteria. Some plasmids contain resistance to certain medicines used to combat bacterial diseases. If such a plasmid is transferred, resistance may be passed to a whole new group of bacteria.

Bacteria also have the ability to pick up DNA fragments left over after others die. If a piece of DNA sticks to a bacterium's cell wall, it may be absorbed.

masses of volvox cells then reproduce by binary fission into new colonies.

Next comes sexual reproduction. A couple of dozen cells in a colony grow bigger and become the equivalent of female sex cells. Others divide and become male sex cells, hundreds in all. The female cells are similar to eggs in animals, the male cells to sperm. Both types of cells enter the watery middle of the colony.

After that, one "sperm" cell enters each "egg" cell to form a zygote. Each zygote forms a cyst around itself. Meanwhile, the rest of the colony falls apart and dies.

A Dangerous Life Cycle

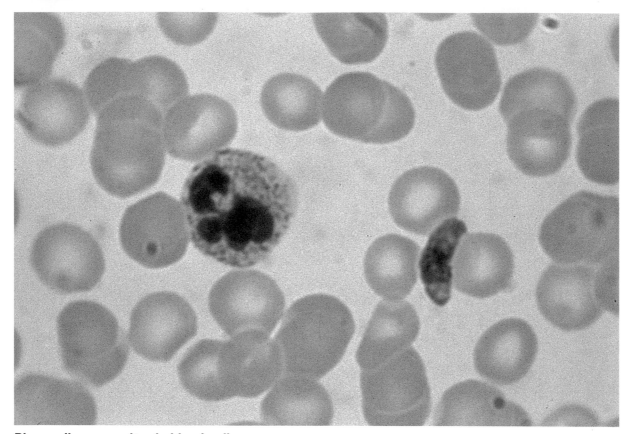

Plasmodium parasites in blood cells

Plasmodium is a protozoan that causes the disease malaria. It belongs to a group known as sporozoans, which are parasites—that is, they feed on an animal's living cells. Plasmodium passes through many stages, during several of which it reproduces in different ways.

Plasmodium spends part of its life in the salivary glands of the Anopheles mosquito. At this stage, the protozoan is round and unable to move on its own. It is called a sporozoite. When the mosquito bites someone, infected saliva travels into the human body and, with it, go the protozoans. They travel through the person's bloodstream to the liver. There they divide, each new protozoan invading a red blood cell.

In the red blood cell, the plasmodium divides again, not in half but into several new protozoans. Eventually, the blood cell breaks open and the protozoans invade new blood cells, where they divide again. The invasion-division-breaking cycle then continues.

Each time the protozoans are released from red blood cells, they produce poisons that cause chills and dangerous fever. After a while, some of the protozoans enter a stage called a gametocyte. At this stage, they can be taken up by a biting mosquito and enter its gut. In the mosquito, the gametocytes undergo changes that turn them into sex cells. They join to form zygotes, which develop into a thread-like form. This form enters the wall of the mosquito's gut and develops a cyst. Next, the protozoan within the cyst divides into thousands of sporozoites. They go to the mosquito's salivary glands and the dangerous cycle starts again.

The zygote remains in a cyst for a year. Then it leaves the cyst and begins to reproduce asexually and form a new colony. Thus, the entire process begins once more.

The volvox colony functions similarly to the body of an animal. The cells in the outer portion of the colony perform functions that are necessary for life. They produce food by photosynthesis and provide locomotion. The reproductive cells cannot make food or feed. Their sole responsibility is to produce the next generation of volvox. Sooner or later, the food-making cells die, much as happens to the body of an animal when it dies. But the reproductive cells have insured that the species survives.

Growth

Like higher organisms, bacteria and protozoans need food and water to grow. For them, growth is simply a matter of getting bigger. Their basic form and organelles do not change.

Conditions in the environment affect the growth of microorganisms, for better or worse. Different microorganisms, for example, require different temperatures and amounts of light to survive. Temperatures above the boiling point kill most bacteria, which is one of the reasons for cooking meat, eggs, and other foods. It is also why boiling contaminated drinking water may prevent bacterial disease.

Prolonged exposure to temperatures lower than the boiling point can also kill bacteria. This fact was discovered by the French chemist Louis Pasteur in the mid-1800s. He found that certain bacteria in food, such as milk, died if they were heated to 145 degrees F. (62 degrees C.) for a half hour and then chilled. The process, which now can be done in seconds, is named pasteurization, after its founder.

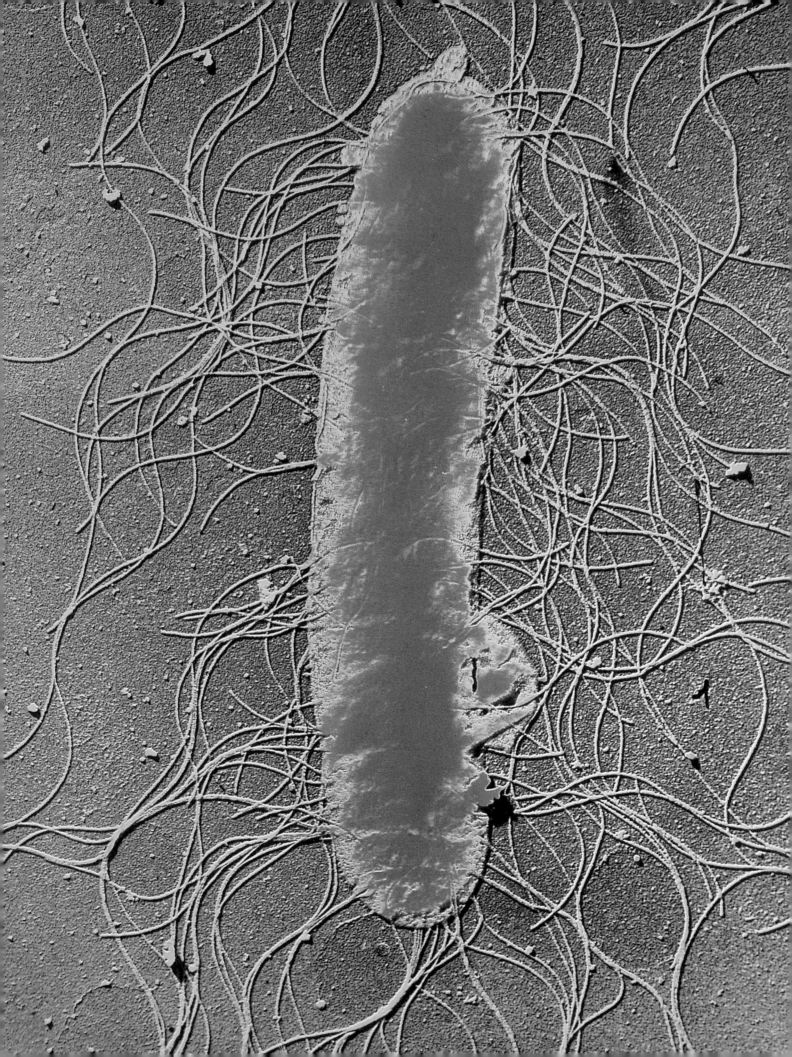

5

Fitting into the Web of Life

 Like higher organisms, microorganisms engage in a constant fight for survival. As they interact with one another and with the rest of the environment, they have an enormous impact on all living things—for better or worse.

The Beginning of the Food Chain

All microorganisms have both enemies and victims. Many protozoans eat other protozoans and bacteria. In most cases, protozoans attack their prey physically, as animals do. In turn, bacteria are eaten by such animals as sponges, and protozoans are eaten by many tiny animals, such as flatworms and the larvae of some fishes. The small creatures that eat bacteria and protozoans are in turn preyed upon by larger ones. Protozoans and bacteria are the first links in many food chains.

Opposite:
Many microorganisms live inside other living things and are a part of many natural processes. This *Proteus mirabilis* bacterium, for example, is normally present in the human intestine, where it feeds on various nutrients.

Chemical Warfare

Since bacteria feed by chemically changing their environment, they are in a constant state of chemical warfare with other microorganisms, including other bacteria. The chemical weapons of a microorganism work only against specific other microorganisms—and no microorganism is itself invulnerable. There is always another organism with weapons that can be effective against it.

For many microorganisms, feeding is also a means of protection. A microorganism that chemically destroys others in its surroundings to defend itself may also nourish itself on their remains. Some microorganisms create a protective chemical ring around themselves. The ring can be seen in the laboratory when they are placed in a colony of bacteria vulnerable to their defenses. The area around these microorganisms becomes clear of bacteria.

Bacteria and Disease

Bacteria cause many kinds of diseases, not just in people but in other animals and plants as well.

Spirochetes, like these, are responsible for Lyme disease in humans. The organisms invade the human body through the bloodstream after a person has been bitten by a tick carrying the bacteria.

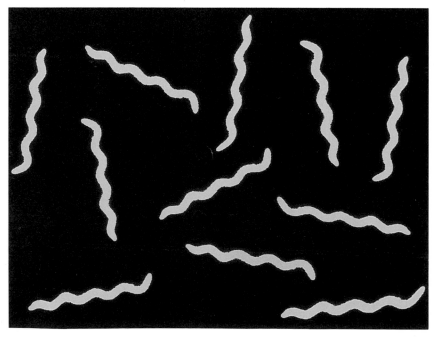

Lyme disease Lyme disease has caused a scare throughout much of North America in recent years. The disease is caused by a spiral-shaped bacterium called a spirochete, which is spread to humans by the bite of certain ticks. The first tick found to carry Lyme disease was the deer tick, which lives in the eastern third of North America. Adult deer ticks feed mostly

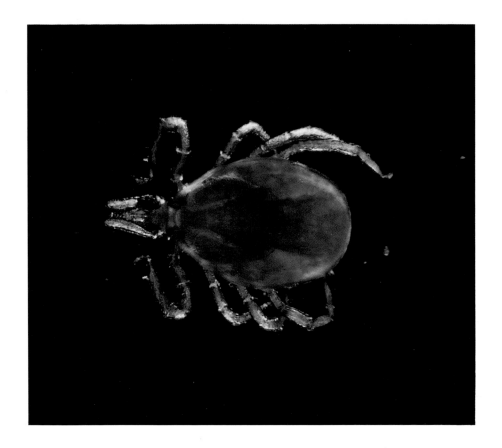

Lyme disease is transmitted through the bite of certain ticks, such as the deer tick, *Ixodes dammini.*

on the blood of white-tailed deer. Lyme disease causes a host of harmful symptoms, ranging from simple aches and pains, to heart and nervous system problems. On very rare occasions, it may be fatal. It can also infect some domestic animals, such as dogs.

Despite the fact that some microorganisms have caused human suffering, the contributions they make to the existence of life on the planet demonstrate that, in nature, everything has its place.

The cycle through which Lyme disease is transmitted is a clear illustration of how bacteria interact with the environment and other living things.

Ticks feed on the blood of birds and mammals by attaching themselves to their host—the animal on which they feed—with their saw-like mouthparts. In the spring, adult deer ticks drop off their host and lay eggs. By early summer, larval ticks hatch from the eggs and look for small mammals on which to feed.

Fitting into the Web of Life

Alien Invaders

Among the enemies of bacteria are viruses. A virus is even smaller than a bacterium. Viruses cause many diseases, including the common cold. They still mystify scientists because they seem to be half living and half nonliving matter. Viruses, which are surrounded by a protein shell, contain nucleic acids, enabling them to reproduce. They cannot reproduce on their own, however. They have to take over a living cell and reproduce within it.

The types of viruses that attack and invade bacteria are called bacteriophages, or phages, for short. Phages are round and have a tubular tail-like appendage tipped with many fibers. When a phage attacks a bacterium, the fibers attach to its cell wall. Each type of phage can attach to only certain kinds of bacteria.

Once it attaches, the "tail" releases an enzyme that dissolves a section of the bacterium's cell wall, creating an opening. Then the "tail" contracts and squeezes the phage's nucleic acid into the bacterium, leaving its protein coat behind. Within the bacterium, new phages—sometimes many hundreds of them—are formed. Eventually the bacterium's cell wall breaks open and the phages are freed.

A phage is partly responsible for the disease diphtheria, which affects the throat, heart, and other important tissues of the human body. Diphtheria is not a viral illness, however. Rather, it is caused by a poison contained in a particular type of bacteria. The bacteria are unable to release the poison until they break open when they are invaded by a phage.

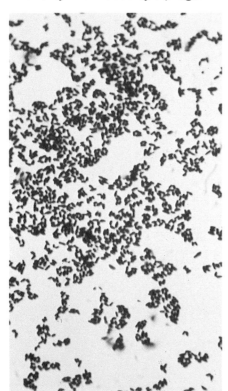

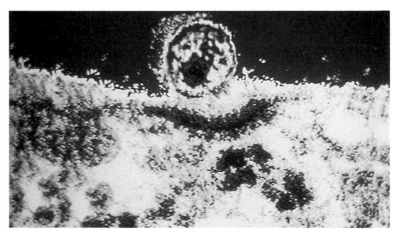

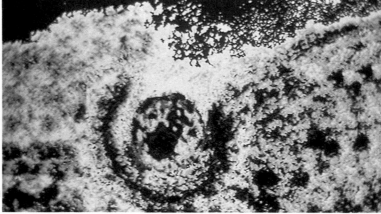

Top: A colony of diphtheria phage.
Right: An HIV virus that causes AIDS penetrates the outer membrane of a human white blood cell.

Most of them attach to white-footed mice and similar rodents. These rodents often carry the Lyme disease bacteria, which enter the larval tick along with the rodent's blood.

By fall, the larval ticks develop into another stage, the nymph. Nymphs do not feed until the next spring, when they again attach themselves to small mammals and, again, may pick up the bacteria. As they grow, the nymphs—and, later, adults—also attach themselves to people. If an infected tick bites a human, it may pass along to that person the bacteria that cause Lyme disease.

Protozoans and Disease

Protozoans cause other diseases besides malaria. One type of amoeba, for example, causes a serious illness called amoebic dysentery. This amoeba forms a cyst as part of its life cycle. When a person ingests food or water containing the cysts, they break open and the freed amoebas attach themselves to glands in the wall of the intestine. There, they feed on blood and tissues, multiplying rapidly.

The invasion of amoebas causes serious abscesses that discharge blood into the intestine and trigger severe diarrhea. Occasionally, the disease can spread to major organs and even be fatal. People who have been infected with amoebic dysentery can pass the amoebas—and the disease—to others through their feces. Amoebic dysentery is common in countries where sanitary facilities are poor.

A flagellate that resembles a worm is responsible for African sleeping sickness. It is transmitted to people through the bite of the tsetse fly, which inhabits wooded areas. Sleeping sickness is fatal unless treated early. Some parts of the African continent are almost uninhabitable because of this disease.

Ultimately, life on Earth would not be possible without the bacteria that fix nitrogen into the soil. Nitrogen is one of the building blocks of organic matter. Although it is present in the air, plants cannot take it from that source. Humans cannot either. Even though you inhale nitrogen in the air you breathe, none of it can be used in metabolism. Your nitrogen comes from eating plants that have taken it from the soil—or from animals that have eaten plants.

Protozoans also cause diseases in animals. One group of sporozoans, for example, afflicts chickens and rabbits with an illness called coccidiosis. It can spread very rapidly among domestic chickens and rabbits, creating severe problems for farmers.

Helpful Microorganisms

Despite the diseases some cause, there are many microorganisms that do far more good than harm. In fact, life as we know it could not exist without them. That's why microorganisms are a vital strand in the web of nature.

Soil makers Bacteria that make soil are among the most important of the microorganisms. They attack dead organic matter and break it down, adding material to soil and releasing nutrients that make it fertile. This process, called decay or decomposition, goes on continually. Old logs, fallen leaves, pine needles, dead animals, and a host of other items are slowly decomposed.

When bacteria cause dead organisms to decompose, they are really recycling chemical elements and compounds essential to all life. Together with heat, solar radiation, and other organisms—such as fungi—bacteria have been recycling the Earth since life began. Carbon, for example, is a building block of all organic compounds. By causing dead things to decompose, bacteria return carbon to a form that once again can be used by living organisms. When bacteria die, the materials of which they are made also return to the environment and are used by other organisms.

Disease fighters Microorganisms can cause disease, but they can also help fight it. The chemicals they produce, and the action of these chemicals on other compounds, are used to make many important medicines, including the "wonder drugs" called antibiotics. Antibiotics are among the most important drugs available in medicine. They are effective in treating many diseases from pneumonia to scarlet fever and dysentery.

The most effective antibiotics come from bacteria and other microorganisms in the soil. In 1949, scientists found a microorganism in a soil sample taken in the Midwest that would later be used to produce an important new antibiotic. The scientific name of the drug is oxytetracycline, but it is produced under many brand names. The microorganism was a kind of actinomycete, regarded by some as a bacterium (others say it is only a close relative). The drug has become one of the most useful in medicine, fighting a host of diseases, including typhus and Rocky Mountain spotted fever. Many other actinomycetes have been used in a wide variety of antibiotics.

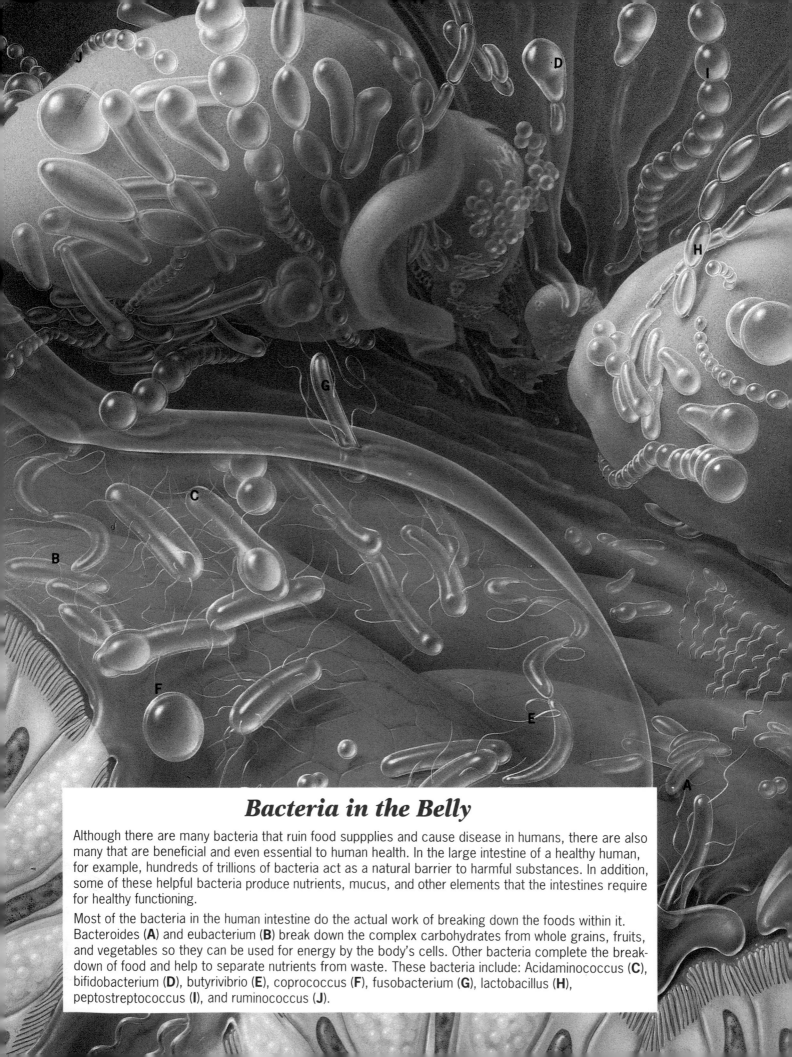

Bacteria in the Belly

Although there are many bacteria that ruin food suppplies and cause disease in humans, there are also many that are beneficial and even essential to human health. In the large intestine of a healthy human, for example, hundreds of trillions of bacteria act as a natural barrier to harmful substances. In addition, some of these helpful bacteria produce nutrients, mucus, and other elements that the intestines require for healthy functioning.

Most of the bacteria in the human intestine do the actual work of breaking down the foods within it. Bacteroides (**A**) and eubacterium (**B**) break down the complex carbohydrates from whole grains, fruits, and vegetables so they can be used for energy by the body's cells. Other bacteria complete the break-down of food and help to separate nutrients from waste. These bacteria include: Acidaminococcus (**C**), bifidobacterium (**D**), butyrivibrio (**E**), coprococcus (**F**), fusobacterium (**G**), lactobacillus (**H**), peptostreptococcus (**I**), and ruminococcus (**J**).

Microorganisms are also valuable in preventing disease. Drugs called vaccines may be made from bacteria or other microorganisms that normally cause disease. Before a vaccine containing these microorganisms is injected in a human, the organisms are either killed or weakened so that they are not harmful. However, the dead or weakened organisms do cause the body to produce antibodies that will protect the human from all future invasions of similar, live, disease-producing microorganisms. Vaccines are given to children at an early age to prevent them from getting serious diseases such as diphtheria, tetanus, and scarlet fever.

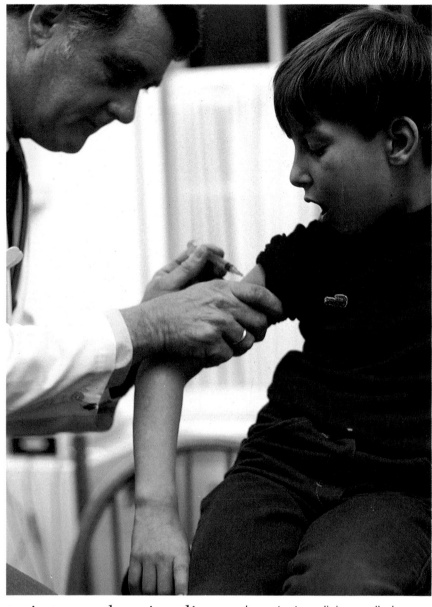

Important medicines called vaccines are made from some microorganisms. Vaccines protect humans from the harmful effects of serious diseases.

Scientists can cause bacteria to produce insulin, a chemical needed by people who suffer from diabetes. Using a technique called genetic engineering, the scientists insert a human insulin-producing gene in a bacterium. When the bacterium divides in two, each organism has a gene that produces insulin. Eventually, millions of similar bacteria form and the insulin is harvested from these microscopic workers and given to humans with diabetes.

Other helpful microorganisms Do you like yogurt and cheese? They are made by the action of bacteria on milk sugar, or lactose, which bacteria change into lactic acid. How about pickles? Bacteria play a key role in the pickling process—as they do in making vinegar and wine.

Foods are not the only products made by bacteria. Chemicals from bacteria are used to soften leather during tanning. Bacterial action on carbohydrates helps form the industrial chemicals butyl alcohol and acetone. Microorganisms also are used in making many vitamins. A bacterium that acts on sugar, for example, produces a chemical from which vitamin C can be derived.

Bacteria and other microorganisms have been used by people for ages to produce useful products. Of course, until microorganisms were discovered and understood, people did not know what processes were involved, only that they worked.

The decomposing and recycling abilities of bacteria have been used effectively in the treatment of sewage. Bacteria break down sewage—not just in major sewage-treatment plants, but in backyard septic tanks as well. Many people with septic tanks treat them with commercial products that increase the numbers of bacteria.

Despite their tiny size, microorganisms are much like all other living things on Earth. Even on their microscopic level, these organisms obtain food, metabolize, reproduce, and react to their surroundings, just as plants and animals do. And although some microbes can be harmful to plants and animals, others are invaluable resources. Whether they are considered "good" or "bad," each microorganism occupies a unique place on our planet. And, though they can't easily be seen, each tiny organism struggles, just as we do, to make a place in the complex but beautiful natural world.

Fitting into the Web of Life

Classification Chart of Microorganisms

The classification of monerans and protists is more difficult than that of other living things. There is much disagreement over how to classify many of the organisms in both kingdoms. Scientists are not even sure how many different species exist. About 2,000 kinds of bacteria are known, but the means for distinguishing species is generally very complicated. There appears to be between 30,000 and 80,000 species of protists, classified in many different ways (different classification systems classify them differently). The following is one common classification for each of the two kingdoms.

Kingdom: Protista

Phylum	Common Members	Distinctive Features
Protozoa	protozoans (parameciums, amoebas, plasmodiums)	one-celled; some have flagella; some have cilia; cannot make their own food through photosynthesis; some are parasites
Dinoflagellata	dinoflagellates	one-celled biflagellates; contain chlorophyll, carotene, and golden-brown pigments; reproduce by binary fission
Euglenophyta	euglenoid flagellates	most are green, one-celled organisms that move with flagella; small, red, light-sensitive eyespot; asexual reproduction
Chrysophyta	yellow-green algae, golden algae	one-celled; many form shells of silica or lime; most have one or two flagella
Bacillariophyta	diatoms	biflagellates; glass-like, silica-coated walls; reproduce by simple cell division and by union of gametes
Rhodophyta	red algae	multi-cellular; undergo photosynthesis; secretions and skeletons contribute to formation of coral reefs
Chlorophyta	green algae	can be single-celled or multi-cellular; resemble higher plants in pigment content and process of photosynthesis; reproduce both asexually or sexually
Cryptophyta	cryptomonads	similar in most ways to dinoflagellates
Phaeophyta	brown algae	multi-cellular; brown pigment that masks the chorophyll; body structure resembles true plants
Gamophyta	conjugating green algae	reproduce in a process that is considered sexual

Kingdom: Monera

Major Groups	Common Members	Distinctive Features
Bacteria	cocci (round-shaped) bacilli (rod-shaped) spirilla (spiral-shaped)	many have a whip-like flagella for locomotion; most reproduce asexually by means of binary fission
Blue-green algae	chroococcales, oscillatoria, nostoc, stigonema	similar in cell structure to bacteria; carry out photosynthesis but do not contain chloroplasts

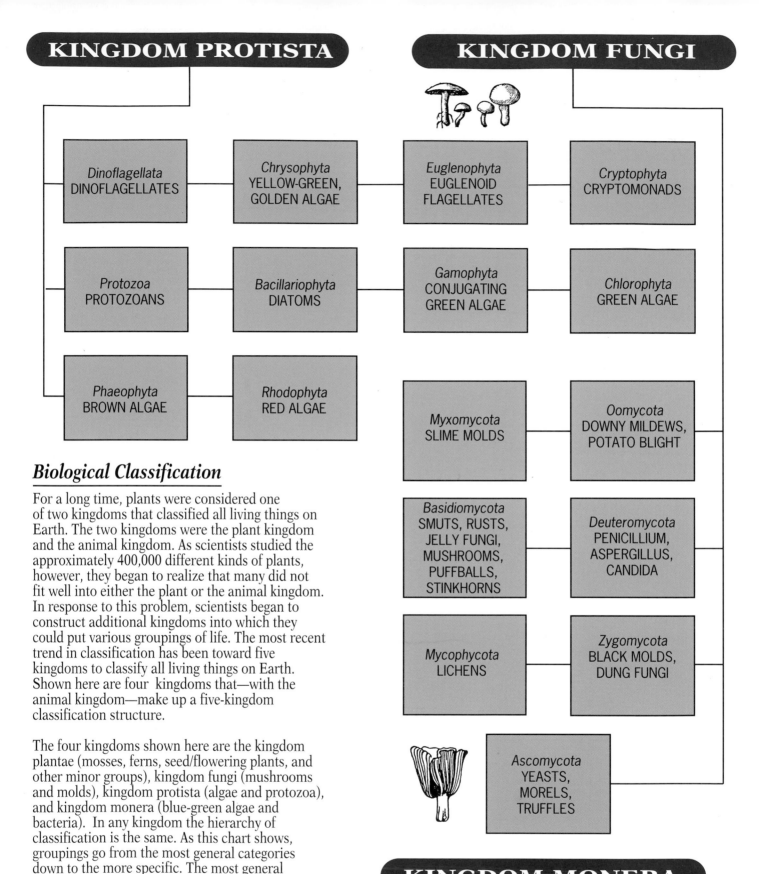

KINGDOM PROTISTA

Dinoflagellata DINOFLAGELLATES	*Chrysophyta* YELLOW-GREEN, GOLDEN ALGAE
Protozoa PROTOZOANS	*Bacillariophyta* DIATOMS
Phaeophyta BROWN ALGAE	*Rhodophyta* RED ALGAE

KINGDOM FUNGI

Euglenophyta EUGLENOID FLAGELLATES	*Cryptophyta* CRYPTOMONADS
Gamophyta CONJUGATING GREEN ALGAE	*Chlorophyta* GREEN ALGAE
Myxomycota SLIME MOLDS	*Oomycota* DOWNY MILDEWS, POTATO BLIGHT
Basidiomycota SMUTS, RUSTS, JELLY FUNGI, MUSHROOMS, PUFFBALLS, STINKHORNS	*Deuteromycota* PENICILLIUM, ASPERGILLUS, CANDIDA
Mycophycota LICHENS	*Zygomycota* BLACK MOLDS, DUNG FUNGI
	Ascomycota YEASTS, MORELS, TRUFFLES

KINGDOM MONERA

Schizophyta BACTERIA, BLUE-GREEN ALGAE

Biological Classification

For a long time, plants were considered one of two kingdoms that classified all living things on Earth. The two kingdoms were the plant kingdom and the animal kingdom. As scientists studied the approximately 400,000 different kinds of plants, however, they began to realize that many did not fit well into either the plant or the animal kingdom. In response to this problem, scientists began to construct additional kingdoms into which they could put various groupings of life. The most recent trend in classification has been toward five kingdoms to classify all living things on Earth. Shown here are four kingdoms that—with the animal kingdom—make up a five-kingdom classification structure.

The four kingdoms shown here are the kingdom plantae (mosses, ferns, seed/flowering plants, and other minor groups), kingdom fungi (mushrooms and molds), kingdom protista (algae and protozoa), and kingdom monera (blue-green algae and bacteria). In any kingdom the hierarchy of classification is the same. As this chart shows, groupings go from the most general categories down to the more specific. The most general grouping shown here is PHYLUM (or DIVISION for plants). The most specific grouping listed is ORDER. To use the chart, you may want to find a familiar organism in a CLASS or ORDER box and then trace its classification upward until you reach its PHYLUM or DIVISION.

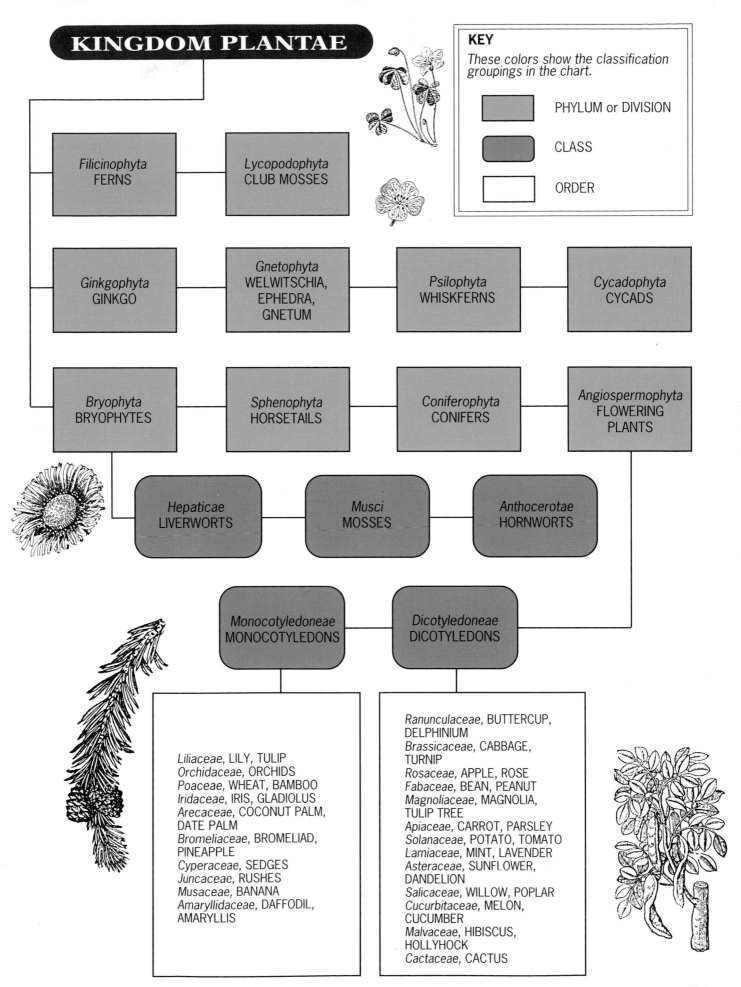

KINGDOM PLANTAE

KEY

These colors show the classification groupings in the chart.

- PHYLUM or DIVISION
- CLASS
- ORDER

Filicinophyta FERNS

Lycopodophyta CLUB MOSSES

Ginkgophyta GINKGO

Gnetophyta WELWITSCHIA, EPHEDRA, GNETUM

Psilophyta WHISKFERNS

Cycadophyta CYCADS

Bryophyta BRYOPHYTES

Sphenophyta HORSETAILS

Coniferophyta CONIFERS

Angiospermophyta FLOWERING PLANTS

Hepaticae LIVERWORTS

Musci MOSSES

Anthocerotae HORNWORTS

Monocotyledoneae MONOCOTYLEDONS

Dicotyledoneae DICOTYLEDONS

Liliaceae, LILY, TULIP
Orchidaceae, ORCHIDS
Poaceae, WHEAT, BAMBOO
Iridaceae, IRIS, GLADIOLUS
Arecaceae, COCONUT PALM, DATE PALM
Bromeliaceae, BROMELIAD, PINEAPPLE
Cyperaceae, SEDGES
Juncaceae, RUSHES
Musaceae, BANANA
Amaryllidaceae, DAFFODIL, AMARYLLIS

Ranunculaceae, BUTTERCUP, DELPHINIUM
Brassicaceae, CABBAGE, TURNIP
Rosaceae, APPLE, ROSE
Fabaceae, BEAN, PEANUT
Magnoliaceae, MAGNOLIA, TULIP TREE
Apiaceae, CARROT, PARSLEY
Solanaceae, POTATO, TOMATO
Lamiaceae, MINT, LAVENDER
Asteraceae, SUNFLOWER, DANDELION
Salicaceae, WILLOW, POPLAR
Cucurbitaceae, MELON, CUCUMBER
Malvaceae, HIBISCUS, HOLLYHOCK
Cactaceae, CACTUS

Glossary

adaptation A body part or behavior that helps an organism survive in its environment.

agar A thick gelatin made from seaweed.

anaerobic Capable of living without oxygen.

asexual reproduction Reproduction that involves only one parent.

binary fission A method of asexual reproduction in which an organism splits in two.

cell The microscopic unit that is the building block of all living things.

cellulose The material of which bacteria walls are composed.

chlorophyll A green substance found in plant cells and some bacteria.

cilia Microscopic hair-like projections on a cell membrane that enable movement.

contractile vacuole The structure in a cell where wastes are excreted.

cyst A hard shell that protects some cells during reproduction.

cytoplasm The protoplasm surrounding a nucleus.

decay The process by which dead organic matter is broken down.

digestion The mechanical and chemical breakdown of food into substances the body can use for growth and energy.

endospore The protective state of some bacteria that allows them to remain inactive in the presence of oxygen.

enzyme A substance that breaks down food.

excretion The removal of wastes that are created during metabolism.

extinct No longer in existence.

eyespot Part of a unicellular organism that is sensitive to light.

flagellum A tail-like structure.

food chain The order in which a series of organisms feed on one another in an ecosystem.

food vacuole The structure in a cell where digestion takes place.

habitat The particular part of the environment in which an organism lives.

metabolism The chemical processes in cells that are essential to life.

nucleus The control center that regulates a cell's activities.

oral groove A channel-like indentation lined with cilia on the surface of a cell.

organelle A specialized structure in a cell that has a specific function.

parasite An organism that lives in or on another living organism.

pasteurization The process by which bacteria are killed through exposure to heat.

photosynthesis The process by which an organism makes its own food.

protoplasm The living matter of cells.

pseudopod A temporary projection of a cell that enables movement.

reproduction The process by which organisms create other members of their species.

species A group of organisms that share more traits with one another than with other organisms and can reproduce with one another.

sperm The male reproductive cell that fertilizes a female egg.

spore A thick-walled, single-to-many celled, reproductive body of an organism.

stimulus A change in the environment that can be detected by an organism.

unicellular An organism consisting of only one cell.

urine A liquid waste produced during metabolism.

vaccine A drug containing weak or dead organisms that is used to prevent disease.

zygote The cell produced by the union of a male and a female sex cell.

For Further Reading

Amdur, Richard. *Chaim Weizmann.* New York: Chelsea House, 1988.

Asimov, Isaac. *How Did We Find Out about Germs?* New York: Walker & Co., 1973.

Bender, Lionel. *Around the Home.* New York: Franklin Watts, 1991.

Donahue, Parnell and Capellaro, Helen. *Germs Make Me Sick: A Health Handbook for Kids.* New York: Knopf Books for Young Readers, 1975.

George, Michael. *Cells.* Mankato, MN: Creative Education, Inc., 1992.

Harris, Jacqueline L. *Communicable Diseases.* New York: Twenty-First Century Books, 1993.

Metos, Thomas H. *Communicable Diseases.* New York: Franklin Watts, 1987.

Miller, Christina G. and Berry, Louise A. *Wastes.* New York: Franklin Watts, 1989.

Nardo, Don. Germs: *Mysterious Microorganisms.* San Diego, CA: Lucent Books, 1991.

Newfield, Marcia. *The Life of Louis Pasteur.* New York: Twenty-First Century Books, 1991.

Nourse, Alan E. *Viruses.* New York: Franklin Watts, 1983.

Silverstein, Alvin, et. al. *Lyme Disease, the Great Imitator.* Lebanon, NJ: AVSTAR Publishing Corp., 1990.

Taylor, Ron. *Through the Microscope.* New York: Facts On File, 1985.

Tiger, Steven. *Diabetes.* New York: Simon & Schuster Trade, 1987.

Wilcox, Frank H. *DNA: The Thread of Life.* Minneapolis, MN: Lerner Publications, 1988.

Wilson, Jonnie. *AIDS.* San Diego, CA: Lucent Books, 1989.

Index